To Mend the World is a wise and wide-awake book about youth ministry. Jason Lief and Kurt Rietema, experienced in their work with young people, recognize that the old ways of youth ministry no longer work. Their approach, in every way one can imagine, is "both-and": both transcendent and immanent, both theoretical and practical, both active and reflective. They see youth ministry as essentially an interpretive task wherein hands-on lived experience and faith claims function in interactive illumination. Their aim is to equip young Christians for an effective, faithful life in the real world, and to help them be knowingly reflective about the menacing, seducing ideologies all around us and committed to creative, imaginative work toward a mended world.

—Walter Brueggemann, William Marcellus McPheeters Professor Emeritus of Old Testament at Columbia Theological Seminary

Jason Lief and Kurt Rietema are two of the boldest and wisest people I know thinking about and doing youth ministry. *To Mend the World* puts this on display in technicolor. The book is deeply thoughtful and helpful. I've been worried that those drawing from innovation theory and social entrepreneurship have not had the patience, attention, and spirit to ask larger theological and philosophical questions to back these practices. However, Lief and Rietema have wonderfully questioned and reworked lessons from these fields of thought. There is much to learn, some things to disagree with, but much more that can bless the minister, young people, and the church in this fine book.

—Andrew Root, Carrie Olson Baalson Professor of Youth and Family Ministry at Luther Seminary and author of *The Church after Innovation: Questioning Our Obsession with Work, Creativity, and Entrepreneurship*

"Youth Ministry is practical theology!" Jason Lief and Kurt Rietema invite us to be facilitators of young people's desires to tackle "adult-sized problems" and bring about change. *To Mend the World* calls us to a better way of doing ministry with youth.
—Dietrich "Deech" Kirk, executive director of the Center for Youth Ministry Training

With a mix of theological reflection, cultural analysis, and storytelling, Jason Lief and Kurt Rietema weave together a compelling account for why youth ministry needs to embrace social entrepreneurship. This is not some mere call for more effective or sustainable ministry. Rather, in social entrepreneurship, the authors see an invitation for youth ministry to rediscover the personal and social transformative encounter that is the beating heart of the gospel. This bold book will challenge assumptions and spark imagination.
—Mark Sampson, author of *The Promise of Social Enterprise: A Theological Exploration of Faithful Economic Practice*

To Mend the World is a collection of principles and experiences reminding us that the original purpose of youth ministry is not to invest in innovating superficial ways of doing church. Instead, it is to create spaces for transformational growth, where young people can develop as changemakers. Their visionary and daring wisdom can lead us out into a broken and uncertain reality, among real people making a lasting difference—something we as a church desperately need.
—Simón Menéndez, lead of Spiritual Changemakers Initiative for the Spanish-speaking world and director of Changemaker Education and Youth, at Ashoka Spain (Madrid)

To Mend the World sets forth a necessary vision not just for youth ministry but for the church! Rich in its theological framework and cultural relevance, Kurt Rietema and Jason Lief reorient our dreams for a younger generation by inviting us to cultivate a much-needed yet missing space: where young people dream, are culturally informed, and act on those dreams to make their communities a better place. In so doing, they demonstrate their faith in Christ's restorative gospel by actively joining him in his ongoing redemptive work in the world.

—Michelle Ferrigno Warren, author of *Join the Resistance: Step into the Good Work of Kingdom Justice*

TO MEND
THE WORLD

TO MEND THE WORLD

A NEW VISION FOR YOUTH MINISTRY

Jason Lief & Kurt Rietema

Fortress Press
Minneapolis

To the motley crew of Old Town—
May you continue to seek human flourishing
in all of your beautifully strange endeavors.
Jason Lief

To Elizabeth, Nancy, Rhiannon, and Zaira—
You inspired it all and continue to make the
world new in the most difficult places.
Kurt Rietema

Contents

.

One

Youth Ministry Must Die

Jason Lief

Early in my teaching career, I met a local pastor for coffee as a way to get connected to the broader community. He was young, with a growing ministry—a pastor on the boundary of hip and culturally engaged. Partway through the conversation, he asked, "Why should I hire a youth pastor?" He wasn't inquiring; his tone suggested hiring a youth pastor is a waste of time. He talked about trends in youth ministry and stereotypes of youth pastors he believed to be problematic. What struck me about the exchange was his willingness to ask the question, Why youth ministry?

The question of the purpose of youth ministry has taken on more urgency as research shows young people are increasingly leaving the church. The response has been a number of books focusing on the nature and purpose of youth ministry, all with important insights to contribute to churches and youth pastors.[1] What gets lost, however, is a conversation about what it means to be the church at this particular cultural moment. This would include not just the issues young people face but the deeper cultural changes that affect the way we think about faith and culture within the framework of secularity.

After all, the purpose of youth ministry, or any form of ministry, is connected with ecclesiology—what it means to be the Christian community at this particular cultural moment.

The dramatic social changes of the nineteenth and twentieth centuries—including a shift from agriculture to an industrial, then a postindustrial way of life—created the social conditions in which youth ministry did its work. The Christian community had to deal with the adolescent—the teenager—and all the anxiety and alienation that came with it. Over the years, there have been enormous amounts of energy and resources devoted to youth ministry. There have been many successes, people who can trace their faith lives to youth events of some type. At the same time, the current cultural moment forces us to confront the question asked by the hip, young pastor: Why should I hire a youth pastor? Put differently, why should a church expect a twentieth-century ministry to address twenty-first-century issues?

It's time for youth ministry to die. Now more than ever, the gospel needs to address the issues young people face. We still need adults who are equipped to live out the gospel with young people as witnesses to God's love revealed in Jesus Christ. The problem is that youth ministry fails to speak to the lived experience of young people. While the packaging has changed, youth ministry remains stuck within a biblical and theological perspective that misses the point. As a result, youth ministry affirms the very cultural trappings it's trying to help young people navigate. This is why youth ministry must die—so it can be transformed.

Death and resurrection are, after all, the heart of the gospel. Yet the gospel is too easily turned into moral and doctrinal programs to help believers go to heaven when they die. The result is a version of Christianity obsessed with believing the right things or living moral lives. Yes, Christian faith is about hope for a life to come, and it should bring about moral transformation. However, to make either of these the primary focus is to miss the point. The death and resurrection of Jesus are not about some abstract spiritualized heaven; the gospel is about transformation. The Holy Spirit doesn't care about our contemporary obsession with growth or progress, as if Christian faith offers some form of a continuous improvement program. The transformation proclaimed in the gospel message about Jesus is a movement from life to death to new life. It's about having an identity deconstructed so God, through the Holy Spirit, can knit us back together. Or to use more traditional theological concepts, it's about justification and sanctification. If this is what the gospel calls us to, then why not allow youth ministry to go through the same process? It's time for youth ministry to die, to be deconstructed, so something new can emerge.

Young people are anxious and increasingly fearful, and many of them are cynical about the future. The cause of this resignation and the problem with current forms of youth ministry stem from a superficial understanding of Christ's death and resurrection that is transactional: Christ's death and resurrection + faith = going to heaven when we die. What's missing in this formula is the biblical understanding that true faith means participating in the death and resurrection of Jesus Christ. Paul says as much in his letter to the Roman church: "For if we have been united with him in a death like his, we will certainly be united with him in a resurrection like his. We know that our old self was crucified with him so that the body of sin might be destroyed, so we might no longer be enslaved to sin. For whoever has died is freed from sin. But if we have died with Christ, we believe that we will also live with him" (Rom 6:5–8 NRSVUE). For Paul, the resurrection was not the resuscitation of a dead body, as if God performed CPR on Jesus and brought him back to life; for Paul, resurrection is something mysteriously new. Resurrection is transformation, a breaking open of the current state of things so a new future is possible. It's much more than the restoration of what was; it's the gathering up of what was to make something new. This is the good news young people need to hear—that in Jesus Christ, God is at work taking the scattered pieces of our lives to make something new.

There's a growing chasm between the biblical message and contemporary North American forms of Christianity. Within the current cultural and political environment, faith tends to be reduced to the affirmation of a way of life. This reduction has contributed to an overspiritualization that emphasizes the universal over the particular. Say a young woman is struggling with loneliness, feeling like she doesn't belong. A pastor can approach this in two ways: (1) by focusing on how God's love is demonstrated in how we love our neighbor, encouraging individuals to enter the lives of others in acceptance and love, or (2) by focusing on how God's love is all we need and that we can be comforted knowing that God is always there for us. Technically, both are true, but one focuses on a particularity (how individuals are called to engage the lived experience of this young person to demonstrate God's love), and the other focuses on the universal (God is always there for us). One is concrete, the other abstract. To overspiritualize is to focus on the universal in such a way that it never intersects with our lived experience. Telling a lonely young person "God is always there for you" does not change their lived experience; demonstrating God's love for a young person by coming alongside them does.

Further, when Christians insist on emphasizing the universal nature of sin and the conversion of the individual sinner at the expense of concrete experiences, the result is unhelpful abstraction. Of course, sin and conversion are biblical and theological truths, but when they're used in opposition to concrete issues, they provide a rationale for not getting involved. This results in the separation of Christian faith from embodied life and an otherworldly Christian spirituality, as faith and cultural life exist on different planes—the spiritual (abstraction) and the temporal (the concrete).

Charles Taylor argued that the difference between the time of the Reformation (the 1500s) and today, in the Western world, is that individuals are less likely to believe the material and the spiritual interact with each other.[2] Put simply, this world is cut off from transcendence. People no longer need to make sacrifices to the gods to ensure a good life; instead, the good life comes through science, technology, and the immanent cultural forces of politics or economics. As the 2020 presidential election showed, people in the West no longer care enough to argue about religion, but they are more than ready to shun family and friends—even resort to violence—over political beliefs. Put simply, the transcendent reality of the divine has been cut off from the daily lives of people living in the West.

This shift in perspective leads to two responses. Some young people see the immanent reality of economics, politics, and science as the ultimate truth—this life is all there is. They reject religion as an archaic holdover from a past time, believing the good life comes through cultural engagement. Meaning and happiness are attainable only through cultural goods, including the accumulation of wealth, success in athletics and academics, and involvement in political and social causes. Increasingly, young people give themselves to these causes with religious fervor, willing to sacrifice and endure suffering for the sake of justice or the election of a political candidate, for example. In this context, faith is transformed from a belief in a transcendent divine reality to a devotion to the cultural forces of the immanent frame. Often, this results in young people abandoning the church.

A second response is for young people to maintain a belief in divine transcendence but see it as something disconnected from everyday life. The spiritual world of faith and the cultural world of embodied life are separate realities. Spiritual beliefs focus on morality and abstract doctrine, while cultural life is guided by the rules and principles of each cultural sphere. While there might be an emphasis on Christian mission and discipleship, this has little to do with the belief that the gospel addresses creaturely life. Salvation, in this context, becomes focused on an entirely different plane of existence—eternal life.

This shift has impacted how young people interact with youth programs in their churches. The first group described opts out of youth ministry or continues to attend merely for social reasons. The second group becomes the focal point of youth ministry, which leads to an emphasis on Christian spirituality disconnected from embodied life. What happens in the athletic arena, in the classroom, and at the workplace has little to do with Christian faith, apart from trite slogans that function as spiritualized virtue signaling. This version of youth ministry doesn't engage the lived experience of young people; it acts to confirm the ways of the world as they exist. Young people show up, listen to messages, participate in activities, and hear about God's love for them and how they should love others, but the gospel message—intentionally or unintentionally—gets reduced to a spiritual form of salvation sometime in the future when we die. Ultimately, youth ministry and the cultural world of young people move along two distinct lines that never intersect—they merely run parallel to each other. Faith becomes focused on a transcendent reality that has nothing to do with this world, and this world has nothing to do with faith.

There is a third way, however, in which divine transcendence and the immanent frame of cultural life intersect. This way has always been the focus of orthodox Christianity, regardless of the historical and cultural moment and the different philosophical tools used to describe it. The task facing the current Christian community, as well as youth ministry, is to reclaim this historic expression of Christian faith while finding a new language to describe it. Young people need to hear the gospel message in a way that addresses their embodied, enculturated lives. They need to hear the political (in a broad sense) message of the gospel that declares the lordship of Christ over all of creation. They need to encounter the triune God, who exists as a divine community and whose love and relationality are the very foundation of creation and human identity. They need to go to the manger, hear the good news about God taking on human flesh in Jesus, and then follow him on the way to Calvary, where the old humanity is put to death, bringing forth the new creation of resurrected humanity, restored and transfigured. They need to hear and see how Christian faith makes a difference *for* this world and *for* their embodied humanity.

The point, after all, is the transformation of our humanity, which is why early Christians insisted on the full humanity of Jesus Christ. Through the early creeds and confessions, they proclaimed that in this human person, full humanity and full divinity were united. Some struggled with this idea that the eternal, unchanging God would or could take on finite human flesh. Clearly, this struggle continues within contemporary Christianity with the tendency toward abstraction. Like some in the ancient world, there remains a belief that the created world must be overcome. For example, the modern obsession with progress reflects this belief. Never satisfied, we strive for what is better, for "excellence," for perfection, believing it's possible to "arrive" if only we could become this or that. The cultural world of young people in North America is steeped in this striving; it demands a constant construction and reconstruction of identity. School, sports, musical performances, social media, jobs—in every area of life, young people are expected to grow, improve, and meet the expectations adults have for them. Not meeting these expectations has terrible consequences, which provide the fuel for fear and anxiety. Sadly, this abstraction has found its way into the church. Youth ministry becomes one more performance, one more place where young people must meet the moral, doctrinal, and spiritual expectations of the adult world.

Author Pete Davis refers to this mandatory performance as the "browsing culture." He argues that there is tension between a "culture of open options" and a "culture of commitment." He uses the metaphor of a large hallway in which there are many different rooms available to us. While no one wants to be locked in a room, he suggests that we're living at a time when many people have difficulty moving out of the hallway. They're afraid of committing to a room—of making a choice—for fear of missing out or making the wrong choice. According to Davis, young people act like browsers, which impacts their view of institutions. He writes, "We tend to distrust organized religion, political parties, the government, corporations, the press, the medical and legal systems, nations, ideologies—pretty much every major institution—and we are averse to associating publicly with any of them."[3] For the Christian community, this fear of commitment can be seen in an emphasis on overspiritualized faith. Then the particularity of the incarnation—that God became a human person, Jesus of Nazareth, at a particular time and place—is lost. The eternal entered and embraced the finite. To live as the new humanity of Jesus Christ is to live as finite human beings in relationship to God and neighbor. This is the good news of the gospel.

For the desert monks, men and women who left society to live lives of single-minded devotion to God, spirituality always included the body. The Christian life was a life of discipline and formation in which the passions of the body could be directed, not obliterated. The purpose of their monastic vocation was not to abandon the world; it was to intercede for the world, to stand in the gap. Father Lazarus, a contemporary monk who lived in the same network of caves as Saint

Anthony out in the Egyptian desert, says that when he prays, the entire world prays through him.[4] Interestingly, when my students are confronted with the spirituality of the Desert Monastics, they dismiss them as abandoning the world. The students insist the monks should be able to live within their networks of relationships and cultural activities and still serve God. They don't need to leave the world to love and follow God. What the students fail to recognize is that in going to the desert, these men and women are finally free to love the world, intercede for it, and actively wait for the transformation of all things. My students don't see that their version of Christian faith, with its focus on going to heaven when we die, is the version of Christianity that does not take this world seriously. The students abandon the Christian hope for the transformation of creation promised in Christ's resurrection. They can't see how it is their own spirituality, with its focus on otherworldly concerns, that is disconnected from this life.

Youth ministry must become less spiritual and more human by helping young people see how, in Jesus Christ, God embraces this created life. Youth ministry must turn away from abstract forms of spirituality in which salvation is some sort of transaction for a future heavenly life by calling young people into a Christian way of life that centers on the particularity of God's love for the world. To do this, youth ministry needs to obliterate the wedge driven between this temporal, created world and spirituality. This begins by helping young people see how the gospel addresses the immanent forces of secular culture (politics, technology, science, economics, etc.) that shape their lives. Youth ministers must help young people recognize how they implicitly (and sometimes explicitly) put their trust in education, athletics, technology, and economics and how they are shaped and formed by the practices associated with these aspects of life. Involvement in these areas has become the foundation for the "good life"—a path to happiness. But these social patterns are not neutral; they are not merely the "real world." The patterns take on lives of their own, functioning according to their own rules. The philosophical word for this is *ideology*. The biblical word for it is *idolatry*.

Ideology is a way of seeing the world that is inscribed within our cultural patterns. Far from neutral, social and cultural patterns are imbued with meaning about what it means to be human and what is of the highest value. Over time, these paradigms shift and change, sometimes gradually, sometimes rapidly. In the Middle Ages, for example, the feudal system had a particular view of the way humans ought to organize their lives together. It was grounded in hierarchy, giving a particular structure to society with each person playing their role in an ordered system. Capitalism challenged this view, replacing it with an emphasis on private ownership, competition, and the destruction of traditional social arrangements. The economic arrangements of a particular culture are not neutral—they are never simply the "way it is." These patterns have consequences; they shape and form the way we inhabit the world and the way we imagine what it means to be human. The problem with youth ministry, and the reason for the crisis, is that youth ministers are not tending to the ideological power of the immanent frame—we do not take seriously the way our imaginations are shaped by these cultural forces. So we invite young people to youth group, play games, have lessons, meet in small groups, and encourage them to commit themselves to Jesus, but we don't address their lived experiences as they are shaped by these cultural patterns. To put it bluntly, attempts at faith formation are short-circuited by the impact of these cultural patterns.

Most youth leaders are committed to helping young people develop a Christian faith, encounter Jesus, and live for God in their everyday lives. Many engage cultural issues to help young people navigate their worlds. Often, however, there isn't time to dig deeper

YOUTH MINISTRY MUST DIE 11

into what Paul refers to as the "cosmic powers of this present darkness" (Eph 6:12 NRSVUE)—the cultural patterns that press upon and shape experiences of the world. A biblical example is found in Acts 16. Paul and Silas are in Macedonia when they encounter a slave girl "who had a spirit of divination and brought her owners a great deal of money" (Acts 16:16 NRSVUE). The oracle of Delphi is the high priestess of the Temple of Apollo at Delphi. Her name was Pythia, which connects with this specific story in Acts, as the text literally says the girl was possessed with the "spirit of Python" (Acts 16:16). This slave girl makes money for her owners by telling people their future. When Paul casts the spirit out, Paul and Silas are dragged to the marketplace before the authorities because "her owners saw that their hope of making money was gone" (Acts 16:19 NRSVUE). They are accused of "disturbing [the] city," which could be read as "disturbing the economy" (Acts 16:20 NRSVUE). Even in Paul's day, it was clear one could believe, act, and say whatever they wanted—just don't mess with the money. Acts 16 speaks to ideology. Of primary concern for these "owners" was not true spirituality, or belief in their gods, but the spirituality of the economy—money. This is what Jesus means when he personifies money in Matthew 6:24: "No one can serve two masters, for a slave will either hate the one and love the other or be devoted to the one and despise the other. You cannot serve God and wealth" (NRSVUE). Money or wealth ceases to be a means of exchange in this passage; it is a powerful force, a god, that shapes and forms our understanding of the world, our relationship to our neighbors, and our view of what it means to be a human being.

This is the question for youth ministry: How do youth leaders address the ideological issues at work in the lives of young people? How do we help young people step out of the spirituality of mammon, the spirituality of wealth that shapes and directs our lives, and step into the new humanity of Jesus Christ? We can do this by helping young people connect Christian faith with their embodied cultural lives. To do this, the Christian community must turn away from the form of spirituality that refuses to contest the ideological forces at work in the world, content to focus on a future world to come. We must contest every form of abstract spirituality that does not see our human identities, made in the image of God, as embodied—the inseparable union of body and soul. This should be done not with metaphors of battle or conquest but with metaphors of creation and resurrection. The last thing the Christian community needs is one more version of a culture war—the point is not to set the Christian community over and against secular culture. The point is to help young people awaken to the reality of God's reconciling presence in this world, to show them that in Jesus Christ, God opens our eyes so we might see what and who God has created us to be. It is then to announce the good news of God's reconciliation of the world, living as signs of this reconciliation as we seek to love God and love our neighbor.

Defining Terms

Entrepreneurship is a form of "creative destruction" for the purpose of bringing about change not by tweaking the current arrangement but by bringing forth something new.[5] At its core, the goal of social entrepreneurship is the disruption of the existing social arrangement. The primary goal isn't to make money but to address unjust or oppressive social situations through economics. Social entrepreneurship is different from social services and social activism. **Social services** are institutions and organizations that address the effects of inequality on the lives of people. These organizations function like hospitals, providing care for people who experience the negative effects of injustice and oppression. Social services do not provide *direct action*, meaning they're not trying to change social and cultural patterns; instead, they provide help and resources to people affected by the inequity of social systems so they can navigate the current system more successfully. **Social activism** describes organizations and individuals who work to mobilize others so they might seek to change the status quo.[6] Social activism seeks change through *indirect action*, meaning the focus is on inviting others to work toward transformation. **Social entrepreneurship** involves *direct action* and *disruption*, working to dismantle the existing system to create a new paradigm.

Most church mission trips fall under the category of social services. Young people work with organizations and/or churches that help alleviate the effects of social problems. Soup kitchens, homeless shelters, and food pantries are examples of social services. They are crucial, but they don't address the systemic, underlying causes of the problem. Some churches and youth groups work to raise awareness of issues. That's social activism. Examples of this are raising awareness of the need for clean water in certain parts of the world or raising money to provide organizations working on the issue with the resources they need. Again, this is very important, but it doesn't actively address the systemic, underlying causes. Social entrepreneurship is utilizing the economic sphere to directly address the systemic, underlying issues that cause particular social problems.

Missional Entrepreneurship

There are two ways of thinking about social entrepreneurship from a Christian perspective. The first merely adopts current forms of business practices, along with their ideological underpinnings, and applies them to a specific social problem. The transformational aspect of this approach is understood as a "double bottom line," meaning the goal of social change is added to the goal of making a profit.[7] The second approach focuses on social change through the transformation of business practices. This approach sees business practices as more than a means to an end; it provides an opportunity to address the hidden, ideological aspects of the dominant economic paradigm that lead to the commodification and objectification of human persons and groups by reducing everything to competition and consumption. A missional approach to social entrepreneurship attempts to reimagine economic participation in a way that seeks human flourishing grounded in the gospel.[8]

The missional approach provides an opportunity for a partnership between social entrepreneurship and youth ministry—helping young people reimagine our economic lives together. Social entrepreneurship is a crucial tool for disruption and recreation. It does this in multiple ways: first, the necessary disruption needed to bring change to a particular social issue, and second, helping young people reimagine human agency and identity as part of a robust theological anthropology.

Social Entrepreneurship and Theological Anthropology

Theological anthropology is an interpretation of the human person in the context of beliefs about God. From a Christian perspective, this means understanding the human person in relation to biblical revelation and the subsequent theological interpretation of Scripture by the Christian community. The opening chapters of Genesis make important claims about humans as image bearers of God within a network of life-giving relationships (God, creation, and our fellow humans). Biblically speaking, these relationships are the foundation of human identity. This is supported by the historical development of the doctrine of the Trinity, which establishes God's identity within the eternal relationship between the Father, Son, and Holy

Spirit. To be made in the image of God, therefore, is to be made in the image of the triune God. Theologically speaking, to be human is to be fundamentally relational.

In this context, the problem of sin is also relational. Throughout the Old and New Testaments, sin is framed as the violation of the covenant—a treaty between God and humanity. The impact of sin, described in Genesis 3, reverberates outward into these relational aspects of human identity. The fracture of the relationship between God and humanity leads to violence (e.g., Cain and Abel) and cultural oppression (e.g., the Tower of Babel) that continue to create problems within contemporary society. The incarnation of God in the person of Jesus Christ provides both a solution to the problem of sin and the fulfillment of human identity. In Christ's death and resurrection, the covenant between God and humanity is restored, leading to the possibility of a new humanity and new creation. It is in the restoration of humanity in Jesus Christ that social entrepreneurship and theological anthropology intersect as our relationship to God and creation is transformed. Through the Holy Spirit, the church takes up the task of participating in God's work of transformation through acts of love. By taking up the cultural tasks that are foundational to living as human beings in the world, the Christian community expresses this love by seeking the flourishing of others and creation. This is where social entrepreneurship can become an important tool for the Christian community to address the social problems afflicting our neighbors as we redefine what it means to live in this world as a human being.

For social entrepreneurship to function in this way, the Christian community must raise awareness of the social problems that perpetuate the cycles of sin and despair. The church needs to recognize the impact of sin on the lives of young people. This means acknowledging that while sin is personal, it also reverberates out into the social and cultural patterns that foster alienation. To address these broader implications of sin, the Christian community must provide a critical engagement of economic life, one that takes seriously the relational core of human identity. A contemporary example of this can be found in Pope Benedict XVI's encyclical *Charity in Truth* (*Caritas in Veritas*), in which Benedict reframes economic life in relation to the irreducibility of the human person, made in the image of God.[9] This means recognizing the ways in which capitalism (or any other ideology) reduces human identity to economics, thus failing to recognize the irreducibility of the human person. According to Mark Sampson, the "ontologically relational" nature of being human means a Christian engagement of economic theory must oppose the reductionist logic of capitalism.[10]

True spirituality isn't to leave this material world behind; it is to be fully alive in relationship with God and all of creation. Humans were created to go out from our own selves, to encounter and care for the creation and our fellow humans. This is the nature of love, and this is what it means to be fully alive in the Spirit—to no longer be turned inward, trying to control and manage the world. Benedict and Sampson recognize how the market flattens the human person, objectifying individuals and communities as they are reduced to its logic. Most young people (and most adults for that matter), if asked, couldn't articulate this. But deep down, they know something's wrong. All the anxiety, the stress, the pressure to succeed, and the palpable fear of failure are symptoms of this great flattening. For many, faith is an add-on, a supplement to help them achieve the good life. The time has come for Christian faith to be more than a guarantee of the life to come; it's time for youth ministry to reclaim the message of the early Christian communities and call young people to wake up and embrace this finite, embodied life. It's time for youth ministry to become less spiritual and more human.

Two

Disconnection

Jason Lief

The 2019 film *Joker* tells the story of how Arthur Fleck transforms into the Joker. The dark and violent film portrays Arthur as awkward and mentally unstable as he seeks help for his troubling thoughts. He works as a clown, saying throughout the film, "My mother always tells me to smile and put on a happy face. She told me I had a purpose to bring laughter and joy to the world."[1] At one point in the film, Arthur sneaks into a theater where the wealthy, high-society people of Gotham are watching Charlie Chaplain's *Modern Times*. This indicates the two films share common themes—the impact of economic patterns on the poor and the important role fantasy plays in supporting the status quo.

A primary theme in *Modern Times* is the importance of work and what happens to those who don't work. Throughout the film, the main characters fantasize about what it would be like to be wealthy. They spend the night in an upscale department store, sleeping in plush beds and trying on expensive clothes. In one scene, the Tramp and a young woman—an orphan—imagine life in a nice, middle-class home where food is plentiful (including a cow that walks by the front door, providing fresh milk for the day) and the domestic roles of housewife and breadwinner are established. All of this is framed within the capitalist ideal of work. The film begins by showing how the industrial factory system mistreats working-class people. As the Tramp moves from absurd situation to absurd situation, he is always trying to find work. The final scenes of the film function as a sort of wish fulfillment: the young woman realizes her dream to be a dancer, and the Tramp finds work as a singing waiter. All of this is short-lived, however, as circumstances force them from their jobs and back on the run. The film ends with an Arthur Fleck–type moment where the Tramp forces a smile on the face of the young woman as they walk off into the sunset, hand in hand.

Arthur Fleck is a Tramp-like character, working as a clown in the economically depressed Gotham. Fleck fantasizes about being a comedian, about having a romantic relationship with a woman living down the hall, about being on a late-night talk show, and finally, about meeting his biological father—who he believes to be Thomas Wayne, a wealthy businessman and the father of Bruce Wayne. Throughout the film, the boundary between reality and fantasy is blurred. An important cue in the film is the iconic stairway that provides one of the more memorable scenes. Every day, Arthur ascends and descends the stairs, moving from fantasy to reality, and then goes back up the stairs to his apartment, where he again inhabits his self-made fantasy world. As these fantasies are ruptured and unrealized, Arthur descends into violence, culminating in his final descent down the stairs as the Joker. Arthur Fleck loses himself in a chaotic explosion of fantasy, unleashing violence on the social world of Gotham. By the end of the film, the boundary between reality and fantasy is erased—all that remains is fantasy. Arthur no longer exists; there is only the Joker.

The current social and cultural situation is one where the transcendent view of God has been replaced with an emphasis on cultural forces like economics, politics, science, and technology. This view contributes to young people abandoning traditional beliefs in God for what are considered more believable cultural narratives. At the same time, it fosters a form of religious dualism in which belief in God provides the guarantee of morality, meaning, and a future life to come but doesn't really address the everyday cultural experience of young people. Both *Modern Times* and *Joker* speak to the powerful influence of these cultural narratives that take on lives of their own. Economics becomes less about how we meet our basic needs for survival and more about constructing a fantasy that provides a way of securing meaning, pleasure, and identity. Politics is less about how we work together to provide solutions to problems and much more about affirming a particular worldview as part of a zero-sum game. The move from transcendence to immanence hasn't eliminated religious abstraction; it has transformed it into new immanent forms of ideology disguised as spirituality.

Youth ministry functions like the stairs in *Joker*. During the week, young people inhabit the cultural forces that shape their identities. Some successfully navigate them, while others struggle. Then they ascend the stairs to church or youth group and hear all about the Christian life—how God loves them, how God has a wonderful future planned for them, and how they're supposed to live for Jesus. Only there's no connection between the two worlds. Just the stairs, back and forth. The fantasy of the one sustains them through the other, but they don't have anything to do with each other. So instead of challenging these cultural forces, we provide young people with an otherworldly form of Christian faith disconnected from their lived experience. Doing so leaves the ideological fantasy untouched, forcing young people to navigate it on their own terms. Youth group gets reduced to one option among others. Adults want youth ministry so our kids will be moral and go to heaven when they die, but should youth ministry address economic, political, or technological issues related to *this* world? To remain faithful to the gospel, the answer must be yes. This means youth ministry must address the ideological fantasies at work in the lives of young people—beginning with economics. This is why youth ministry needs social entrepreneurship.

The Pocket God

Back-Pocket God is the culminating work of the National Study of Youth and Religion. The book consists of interviews with participants ten years after their initial conversations. Now in their late twenties, their experiences and life trajectories are diverse. Some remain committed to religious belief, while others have solidified their unbelief. Most live in a quasi-committed in-between, demonstrating basic religious beliefs and experiences but holding them loosely and vaguely. When directly asked about what they believe, most provide a basic rundown of generic Christian beliefs about the Bible, salvation, sin, and heaven and hell. But these beliefs are not central to their lived experience or their identities.[2]

In reflecting on the conversations, the authors of *Back-Pocket God* reaffirm past themes of emerging adulthood and the markers associated with it. A primary focus is the importance of meaningful work—the type of work that allows people to make a difference in the world.[3] The authors found that work was essential to finding purpose and meaning and ultimately to being happy. They write,

> Across our interviews, regardless of how religiously committed young adults were, the idea of work contributing to their personal sense of meaning and purpose was frequently expressed. For the most religious informants, this was often, though not always, an obvious outgrowth of their faith or spiritual practice. For the less

religious or nonreligious, work may be functioning as an alternative source of meaning in the absence of religiosity. For most emerging adults, regardless of their relationship with religion, work—or the desire for work—was a key part of their identity. Work not only signals that they are responsible and committed people but also serves as a source of meaning and fulfillment in their lives.[4]

While work is clearly a means for identity, meaning, and making a difference in the world, the authors find that religion is less impactful. While their research reveals two groups—one committed to religious belief and the other moving into the nonreligious category—overall, they suggest religion doesn't inspire either group in the way it did for past generations. They write, "As such, religion remains a theoretical or abstract option for them, but it doesn't have the pull or attraction to really grab their attention as something to which they would fully commit."[5] Ultimately, their conclusion is that religion increasingly isn't important for emerging adults. They hold on to a vague spirituality—most believe in god, but it's a god that's far removed from the center of everyday life, reduced to what they call a "pocket God" who serves "their own idiosyncratic needs and desires."[6]

These findings are what you'd expect when religious belief gets disconnected from human experience. Increasingly, as other areas of life become more meaningful and robust, spirituality and religion are relegated to merely being one more aspect of human life among many others. For many, religion is not even the most important, even if it's never jettisoned. These findings demonstrate how the economic sphere of life—the life of work and finances—has become *the* sphere in which meaning, identity, and even social transformation happen. God becomes an add-on, a moral guarantee, an additive that provides the affirmation of a particular way of life but has very little to do with this life. The result is that identity, embodied life in this world, is shaped more by the narratives of these particular spheres than it is by the gospel.

Spiritual Capitalism

Interpreting economics as a contemporary form of spirituality is an important first step for youth ministry, as it addresses the lived experience of young people living in the West. An important contemporary voice on this issue is Kathryn Tanner, whose current work focuses on the spiritual power of capitalism and how it shapes individuals and communal identity as it presents a particular view of meaning and worth as the ultimate truth about the good life. Every area of life comes under the influence of progress, efficiency, and demand as subjects are forced to "completely identify [themselves] with [the market]."[7] The religious nature of capitalism can be seen in its internal logic, in which merits and grace function to determine who is in and who is out. Money functions as the means of grace that determine one's status, but in this economy, the means of grace are gained through competition by creating and re-creating one's identity through continuous cycles of formation. At the heart of this process is the creation of a brand that increases desirability, that allows one to be consumed. Here takes place an accelerating cycle of justification, where identity is deconstructed to overcome sin—the flaws that make one undesirable—and sanctification, where identity is reconstructed in ways that allow one to be properly consumed. But this salvation is not once and for all; it is a continuous, never-ending process of identity construction and deconstruction.

This capitalist spirituality disciplines our imaginations and shapes our lived experience. It even conditions the way we participate in religion, seeing it as one more field in which to compete for power and status. As philosopher Zygmunt Bauman writes, "Becoming and remaining a sellable commodity is the most potent motive for consumer concerns, even if it is usually latent and seldom conscious, let alone explicitly declared."[8] This spills over into the church and into youth ministry, as it becomes one more field in which young people compete—working to meet the religious expectations of adults. The gospel message is lost as it is abstracted from the lived conditions in which young people compete to construct their identities. The cultivation of faith in a radically transcendent God somewhere out there is good preparation for a spiritualized world that exists in some distant eternal future. The embodied lives of young people are left to the mercies of the capitalist spiritual formation—what some might even refer to as the "real world."

The ideological and spiritual impact of capitalism on the lives of young people is not just a discussion among theologians and philosophers; it is also an important part of understanding the social and cultural formation of young people. Journalist and cultural critic Malcolm Harris explores this in his book *Kids These Days: Human Capital and the Making of Millennials*. He describes a world based on constant change at faster and faster speeds, where the dominant rhetoric directed at young people is about preparing for a changing world, for new forms of labor, and for the development of skills fit for a twenty-first-century workforce. His primary claim is that regardless of the way this rhetoric is packaged, the primary way that industry, the government, and the broader social world understand young people is "as investments, productive machinery, 'human capital.'"[9] The result is a constant state of anxiety as young people lose whatever little agency they had.[10] Harris presents a cultural world in which young people are initiated into competition at an early age through a school culture "built around hyper-competition."[11] While this prepares them for the workforce, it comes at a price: anxiety, depression, and a fear of failure.

Human identity, in this context, is marked by developing the skills to navigate this reality. It means being able to successfully compete by constructing an identity that is easily consumable through social media. Basically, we're asking young people to create platforms for their identities—who they think they are and who they want to become. Adults feed this process by focusing on the concern that young people will fail to "meet the demands of a changing world," which leads to a belief that young people are in constant need of an "upgrade."[12]

What Harris describes are the consequences of an economic vision of human flourishing that has fostered what he refers to as "Xtremely Sad Teens." He writes, "American kids and teens, across race, gender, and class lines, are spending less time doing things that make them happy . . . and more time doing things that make them especially unhappy."[13] Put simply, the question of what it means to live as a human being—what human flourishing looks like—is given an economic and technological response. This vision of reality, however, is an unattainable fantasy undergirded, supported, and perpetuated by social and cultural institutions. The result is the formation of young people who are anxious, depressed, and increasingly unhappy.

This analysis suggests Karl Marx was right about some things. He recognized how capitalism informs how people imagine what it means to be human. Marx was right about the way religion can function as an "opiate of the masses," anesthetizing people so they accept the status quo. The founder of liberation theology, Gustavo Gutiérrez, understood how religion was being used to encourage people to ignore their pain and suffering. He saw how theology became focused on high-minded concepts and principles that did little to change the lives of the people. He insisted that theology and religious experience begin with the concrete experience of people—with their suffering. The gospel is not good news about a future reward; it's good news about how the death and resurrection of Jesus Christ bring the transformation of the kingdom of God to this world—to this time and space. This isn't social gospel—it's just gospel.

The problem facing youth ministry is similar. All the programming, teaching, social activities, and focus on mission work are good and well-intentioned. Most youth pastors, if they're honest, admit to feeling the tension between the gospel and the lived experience of young people. They recognize the forces that are pulling young people in different directions. They are also aware of the "pocket God" phenomenon that occurs as social and cultural pressure force faith to the periphery of their lives. A well-known and legitimate complaint from youth workers is about all of the things that compete for the time and attention of young people. What gets missed, however, are the deeper social and cultural forces at work. Youth workers respond to this dilemma by trying to make programming better. They work harder to connect, to make it interesting, many often searching for the next wave or popular approach to bring resolution. The move to individual and personal spirituality and piety makes sense; it provides a space for youth ministry and church to speak apart from the pull of these other forces. Unfortunately, this spiritualization can easily end up mimicking the economic paradigm young people are already conforming to. In this context, spirituality and the markers of the spiritual life (morality, piety, doctrinal knowledge) become one more competitive arena—one more area in which young people make themselves consumable by the adult world.

Jesus Is Tricky like That

A favorite movie at my house is the *Hunt for the Wilder People*, based on the book *Wild Pork and Watercress* by Barry Crump. The film tells the story of Bella and Hector, who take in a foster teen named Ricky.

An early scene in the film shows Ricky and Hector at Bella's funeral. The pastor gives a brief sermon:

> **PASTOR:** You know sometimes in life it seems like there's no way out. Like a sheep trapped in a maze designed by wolves. If you're ever in that situation there are always two doors to choose from: the first door, oh it's easy to get through, and on the other side all the nummiest treats you can imagine: Fanta, Doritos . . . burger rings, Coke zero. But you know what, there's also another door. Not the burger ring door, not the Fanta door, another door that's harder to get through. Guess what's on the other side?
>
> **RICKY BAKER:** Vegetables?
>
> **PASTOR:** No, not vegetables.
>
> **OLD WOMAN FROM THE BACK:** Jesus?
>
> **PASTOR:** You would think Jesus. I thought Jesus the first time I came across that door. Not Jesus. It's another door. And guess what's on the other side of that door?
>
> **OLD WOMAN FROM THE BACK:** Jesus.
>
> **PASTOR:** Jesus, yes Jesus. He's tricky like that, Jesus. So let us pray, to Jesus, please to make it a bit easier to get through those doors and to find you and your bounty of delicious confectionery.[14]

The problem with this sermon is that it doesn't make much sense. What does it mean to encounter Jesus? In a similar way, youth leaders often use abstract principles and ideas to answer this question, usually ending with a superficial, often moralistic application. We emphasize teaching and preaching in ministry because we assume if we give people the right ideas, somehow these ideas will be applied and bring transformation. Unfortunately, these spiritual ideas never address the lived experience of young people—the same way the sermon of the pastor did not address the lived experience of Hector or Ricky. The approach to spirituality through the abstract doesn't help them engage the more pressing question, What does it mean to be human? Or how do the death and resurrection of Jesus Christ lead to a new way of being human in the world right now, and what does this mean for my life?

A More Human Youth Ministry

Youth ministry needs to address the humanity of young people. To do this, youth ministers need to cultivate a robust theological anthropology or think about what it means to be human. Theological anthropology involves a conversation about the role of culture in identity formation. Culture isn't just the neutral environment in which humans live, nor is it something evil that Christians need to avoid. The problem with the "in the world but not of the world" approach is that no one stops to define what we mean by "the world." Humans are cultural. We're immersed in culture, and we're shaped by it. Try thinking without language; try praying without the concepts provided by our cultural context. Culture provides the building blocks for human consciousness. Seeing culture as a place of temptation is much too simplistic; so too is seeing it as just neutral stuff that is neither good nor bad. Yet there's a tendency within the Christian community to approach culture from the standpoint of either neutrality or temptation.

Consider the nature of human consciousness—the "I" from which we understand ourselves in relation to the world. The Christian tradition has historically called the center of human life a *soul*, something that is nontemporal and nonmaterial and goes on living after we die. Body/soul dualism is grounded in a belief that bodily life, including culture, is temporary, while the spiritual soul is eternal. This belief makes the soul, or the spiritual, more important, which then leads to a de-emphasis of our bodies. I often ask students whose primary language is not English what language they think and dream in. For someone who has never lived in a different culture, it seems like a strange question. But when they hear their classmates talk about the strange experience of thinking and dreaming in one language, then in both languages, only to finally switch over to English, they're amazed. Language plays an important role in shaping both our view of the world and our understanding of the self, or the "I." Which means our souls, whatever and wherever they might be, cannot be easily disconnected from our cultural lives. Our embodied lives shape us in ways we're not usually aware of. More often than not, our ideas are shaped and birthed out of our cultural experiences. We grow up in communities that teach us language, most of the time learned by copying the words we hear around us. We engage in the cultural patterns of work, religion, play, and community long before we ever begin attending school. These patterns shape and form our understanding of the world around us, which gives us the language and categories to construct the "I" or "soul"—our identities.

This idea can be controversial. The debate between what are called *structuralism* and *realism* is often a debate about the role culture plays in shaping identity. This plays out in politics with conversations about gender and race. In the Christian community, it lurks beneath the understanding of sin and salvation. People on the structuralist side believe culture plays a central role in shaping identity and meaning. They tend to focus on things like social transformation, social justice, and more recently, critical race theory. On the other hand, those who hold a more realist perspective focus on the personal nature of the individual that transcends culture. They insist the gospel not be reduced to social transformation. Instead, they see it as being about the transformation of the individual—what they might refer to as the "heart." They might not be able to say exactly where the "I" is, but it's real, and it is this "I" that God loves and saves.

Ministry changes depending on which of these two perspectives a person holds. Is the focus of youth ministry identity construction and social transformation? Or is the focus of youth ministry to help young people come to a saving belief in Jesus Christ? It seems most youth ministry focuses on the latter, creating the conditions in which the cultural lives of young people are reduced to doctrinal and moral teachings. As previously discussed, the problem with this is it causes the gospel to run parallel to the lived cultural experience of young people. The gospel is about the salvation of the individual, the soul or "I" that is distinct from cultural life. Cultural life only matters when it comes to this personal salvation; from a moralistic perspective, it is something that leads people astray and tempts them to sin.

At the heart of this discussion is the question of the relationship between lived experience and abstract ideas. Those who hold a more realist perspective think the focus of youth ministry is to provide the right beliefs that address the individual at the "heart" level. These aren't necessarily deep philosophical or theological belief systems; most youth pastors are much more relationally and experientially focused. This perspective emphasizes the need for young people to have the right ideas. Giving them the right theology or worldview becomes the means for personal transformation and salvation.

Those who hold a more social constructionist perspective will focus on the influence of cultural patterns—or social structures—in shaping the way young people think about the world. The focus here is to recognize how people's identities and perspectives are shaped by the way language and social patterns structure the world. The focus is on changing the way people interact with the social world. Ideas or worldviews flow from the way one lives, not the other way around. Though it seems like ideas about the world are simply "the way things are," this reality is socially constructed. Change the cultural patterns and it changes the way people think about the world. The reemphasis on liturgy and spiritual formation in Protestant churches and in youth ministry pushes in this direction. The focus isn't to change how we think but to change our practices—how we inhabit the world. By changing how we live, formed and shaped by liturgical practices, our minds become attuned to God and a new way of life grounded in the death and resurrection of Jesus Christ.

Embodied practices, including our concrete cultural patterns, do much more to shape who we are and how we live than our rational thoughts. In *Good Habits, Bad Habits: The Science of Making Positive Changes That Stick*, author Wendy Wood claims that most of our identity and behavior is not influenced by what she calls "executive control functions"—our sense of agency, willpower, and decision-making. Instead, she argues that many parts of our lives are "stubbornly resistant to executive control." [15] While people assume that identity is primarily shaped by the rational ideas that inform our decision-making process, Wood argues that identity is much more shaped by a "vast, semi-hidden nonconscious apparatus . . . that ultimately runs on its own, without all that much meddling from executive control." [16] Thus, focusing on how we live, not just what we think, has much more potential for bringing about lasting change.

Human identity is not merely the result of socially constructed processes, nor is human identity grounded solely in some immaterial soul. Rather, to be human is to be paradoxically both. The more significant issue has to do with the relationship between culture and human identity and what this means for youth ministry. Focusing on human beings as rational agents who attune their identities to the "real world" is to affirm a realist approach to truth and human identity. Emphasizing the formative power of cultural discourses to structure and restructure reality affirms a social constructionist approach. The problem with realism is it tends to downplay the formative power of cultural discourses. The assumption is that humans have personal responsibility and freedom to act, which overrides the influence of culture. Furthermore, those who hold this position tend to believe that humans create culture; therefore, human freedom and agency are what shape human identity. In youth ministry, this manifests itself in the belief that giving young people the right ideas, doctrines, and worldviews will shape their identities and allow them to transform culture. Personal salvation, a personal relationship with Jesus, and personal faith bring about a transformed individual that can then act in the world.

The problem with social constructivism is it downplays the freedom and agency of human beings, leaving them subject to the formative power of cultural discourse. Because it believes that there's nothing outside the text, meaning our experience of the world is mediated by language, it raises questions about freedom and agency. If language already structures my experience of the world, is it possible to even step outside these cultural discourses? And if it's not possible, then what I perceive to be freedom and agency are limited, as I'm caught within the symbolic world of cultural discourse. My identity is given to me by the community, from outside myself, mediated through language and practices. Truth, in this context, is discursive. It is not a representation of the "real world" out there because I can never get to that "real world" apart from language. (That there is nothing outside the text doesn't mean there isn't a world out there; it means I can't get to it because I'm caught up in language.) The problem with this approach is it undercuts any sense of agency and freedom for the human person. In youth ministry, this can be seen in the way cultural ideologies are uncritically adopted on both the conservative and progressive sides. The current tension within the Christian community over issues of gender and race is influenced less by a biblical and theological approach and more by the adoption of cultural narratives that are believed to be the truth about the world. The conservative conflation of biology and gender is met with resistance from the discourse of progressive ideology, and critical race theory is countered with "all lives matter." Which raises the question: What is the relationship between human agency and cultural discourse?

From a biblical and theological perspective, the human person is irreducibly both body and spirit—an interplay of agency and cultural discourse. Our understanding of reality is given to us by the communal narratives that shape our identities. Language structures and mediates our experiences of the world in such a way that we assume them to be the truth about reality. However, there remains a human person that transcends language and cultural discourse and provides the foundation for human agency and freedom. From a Christian perspective, this is grounded in the resurrection of Jesus Christ. In Luke 24, the disciples are on the road to Emmaus. As they're walking, the resurrected Jesus joins them, only the disciples don't recognize him: "Jesus himself came near and went with them, but their eyes were kept from recognizing him" (Luke 24:16). They're upset about the events that had just transpired, how Jesus was tried and crucified: "But we had hoped he was the one to redeem Israel." Jesus responds by unpacking the biblical story, trying to help them "see" rightly. But it's not until Jesus breaks the bread that their eyes are finally opened and they see Jesus.[17]

So why don't they recognize Jesus? Clearly, their imaginations had been shaped by the cultural narratives of their community. Their understanding of Jesus had been conditioned by political, religious, and social discourses that prevented them from "seeing" Jesus. Their expectations and understanding of Jesus did not include resurrection—at least, not this form of resurrection. So they couldn't see it was Jesus walking with them along the road. It's not until Jesus performs the sign of breaking bread, a central part of his ministry in Luke's Gospel, that their eyes are opened. The resurrection life of Jesus is beyond the cultural discourses of these two disciples. In the same way, the resurrection life of Jesus transcends the cultural discourses of our own lived experience. As Paul says, we are called to participate in the death and resurrection of Jesus Christ: "Do you not know that all of us who were baptized into Christ Jesus were baptized into his death? Therefore we were buried with him by baptism into death, so that, just as Christ was raised from the dead by the glory of the Father, so we also might walk in newness of life" (Rom 6:3–4 NRSVUE). Cultural discourses are real, and they are powerful. So powerful they led to the crucifixion and death of Jesus Christ. But the life that God gives, the life that is the foundation of our human identity, transcends these cultural discourses. This is what Christians are called to participate in—death and resurrection. The cross ruptures the power of these discourses, creating space for human agency and identity grounded in the resurrection of Jesus Christ.

Human identity is shaped by cultural discourse, as we inhabit a world that is mediated by language. At the same time, the Christian life is a call to a constant dying and rising. But as Paul says in Romans 12, "Do not be conformed to this age, but be transformed by the renewing of the mind, so that you may discern what is the will of God—what is good and acceptable and perfect" (v. 2 NRSVUE). We shouldn't think about this in a dualistic sense; this isn't about the material world being bad and some future heavenly world being good. Rather, it's about how the patterns of this world, the discourses of this world that are focused on power and violence, no longer define us. Christians are called to participate in a new form of life, one that transcends the old way of life through the Word God speaks in Jesus Christ.

Identity is shaped by cultural discourses that mediate our experience of the world. We cannot simply ignore them or pretend they're not real; the ministry of the church is a ministry in the midst of our lived experiences. Yet the gospel reminds us that our humanity is not determined by these discourses; our identity is grounded in the resurrection life of Jesus Christ that transcends the cultural patterns of this world. According to theologian Jürgen Moltmann, we participate in the surplus of resurrection that throws open the possibility of a new future, one no longer determined by the past.[18]

Why This Matters

The Western world has lost connection with the transcendence that provided the basis for belief in God and Christianity—what Charles Taylor calls the "immanent frame." Now we live in a time when the immanent cultural forces of politics, technology, science, and economics are seen as the basis for human life. While people still hold on to a belief in God, primarily because they feel some nostalgic need for God to determine ultimate meaning and provide a foundation for morality, increasingly, our faith is placed in the discourses of these immanent social forces. It used to be that people hated and took up arms against other groups because of religious differences; now the primary source of division, in the United States anyway, is political. During the pandemic, political and scientific discourses polarized the United States in ways that religion once did. Discourses have been given a religious spin, but this has less to do with actual religious belief and is more an example of how these cultural forces have fundamentally replaced religion.

Therefore, youth ministry must take these cultural discourses seriously. At this historical moment, the cultural discourses are framing reality for both conservatives and progressives. Young people and emerging adults are increasingly shaped by these cultural forces, with the most dominant one being economics. Capitalism has become the dominant discourse undergirding the institutional lives of young people. Every day, they are bombarded with messages about jobs, competition, branding, and so on. Increasingly, they are encouraged to participate in the capitalist emphasis on commodification, abdicating their responsibility as human creatures to love and care for others. Young people are left to construct and reconstruct their identities in the rapidly changing conditions of the market, making themselves acceptable and consumable by others, including the adult world.

The proper response of youth ministry to this situation is not withdrawal from the world or spiritual dualism, nor is it cultural accommodation. It is an approach that recognizes the significance of economics for human life and that to live as a human being in the world is to necessarily and inescapably be involved in meeting our needs through work. At the same time, it must be an approach that is grounded in a belief that human identity transcends economics, must never be reduced to a commodity, and is always much more than the product of economic discourse—in this case, the language and conceptual framework of capitalism. From a biblical and theological perspective, youth ministry must engage this issue from the perspective of the death and resurrection of Jesus Christ, providing a critique of the dehumanizing aspects of capitalist discourse while also affirming the economic sphere as a place where human agency can foster human and creational flourishing.

Youth ministry does this by developing a robust theological anthropology, helping young people embody what it means to be human from the vantage point of Easter morning.

Three

Reconnection

Jason Lief

Ladybird tells the story of Christine McPherson, a senior at Immaculate Heart of Mary Catholic High School for young women in Sacramento, California. She goes by the self-given name "Ladybird," a source of contention with her mother. Everything about Ladybird's life is pointed elsewhere. She hates living in Sacramento and is determined to attend an elite college on the East Coast, where she'll be able to experience "culture." Her family struggles to make ends meet. Her father has recently been laid off, and her brother and his girlfriend live with the family as they try to find better jobs.

Place is an important theme in the film—Ladybird wants to live anywhere but Sacramento and can't understand why her family has settled for the life they have. Her desire is always for something more, something beyond what's in front of her. She fantasizes about what having sex is like, only to be disappointed when it happens. She tries to upgrade her friend group, alienating her best friend in the process, only to realize the shallow, selfish perspective of her new group. Throughout the film, we see the sacrificial love of her father, who interviews for the same job as his son, then steps aside so he can begin his career. We see Ladybird's mother tending to those who struggle with mental illness, comforting Ladybird's theater teacher, who is struggling with sadness and depression. Driving is central to the film—it opens with the car ride back from a college visit, where the push and pull between Ladybird and her mother is established. Later, we see Ladybird's mother driving home from work on a familiar stretch of highway with the windows down, a drive she treasures as she embraces the beauty of the place she lives. When Ladybird gets her license, she ends up driving the same stretch of highway, finally able to appreciate what she had failed to see before.

The story ends with Ladybird leaving for college on the East Coast. After a night of heavy drinking, she ends up in the hospital. As she walks home the next morning, she comes across a church, where she hears singing. She enters and listens, reflecting on her time at her high school, Immaculate Heart. Out on the sidewalk, she calls her mother and leaves a message on her phone, using her given name—Christine. By reclaiming her name, she reconciles with her past, setting aside the fantasy that prevented her from noticing the beauty and love around her. She finally embraces her family, friends, and the place that shaped her identity.

I show this film to my students to help them understand how the gospel confronts the human desire for an ideal world in the great beyond. In Jesus Christ, God takes up residence in this world as a particular human person to show us what it means to be human. While humanity tries to live into some idealized version of identity, God comes as the suffering Christ. As Adam and Eve attempt to transcend the boundaries of the human condition by eating from the tree, in Jesus Christ, God puts this fantasy to death on the cross, calling humanity to live as finite creatures. Ladybird represents this temptation to seek identity and meaning in some abstract fantasy that declares the finite world we inhabit is not good enough. Her desire is for something more, to the point that she misses the beauty and goodness of the people and places she assumes she knows. The gospel undermines every cultural ideology, every fantasy, that entices us to always want more, to want something else, to constantly become dissatisfied with this finite life and seek something much more abstract, more ideal, more "spiritual."

When the Christian community fails to recognize the power of cultural ideology, particularly the way capitalism frames our experience of the world, we fail to see how young people are conditioned for this anxious longing for something else and something more. Instead of confronting this perspective, youth ministry tries to help young people survive it and possibly even thrive in it. Moral and doctrinal teaching, the call to follow Jesus and commit one's life to him, and the call to evangelism assume young people, if equipped with the right teaching and method, can be witnesses for Jesus as they navigate this way of life. The pervasive nature of capitalism, however, makes this nearly impossible. The lives of young people get caught up in the endless cycle of production, branding, and consumption. Their testimony is predicated on success, so they strive to become the successful athlete, student, musician, or employee that serves as a sign of God's faithfulness and the foundation for their Christian witness. Sometimes failure can be part of this narrative, but only when the young person has recovered sufficiently to integrate it into the testimony of their success. You know, the testimony that goes something like "I once did [fill in the blank], but then Jesus saved me, and all is well." This is a form of Christianity co-opted by capitalism. Grace is not freely given; it's conditional on meeting the cultural markers of success. In the Protestant tradition—though we claim to be saved by grace through faith, not by works—young people need to work hard to demonstrate the conditions of this grace by meeting every cultural expectation.

Like Ladybird, many young people believe their human identity is found out there somewhere, in some abstract fantasy that entices them to become more beautiful, more sexual, wealthier, and more successful. In the church, this can manifest as an obsession to become more spiritual. Like Ladybird, young people need to have this fantasy ruptured so they can claim their names, embrace their finite humanity, and rest in who God is calling them to be. This is an important part of the gospel message for young people—in Jesus Christ, God comes to give our humanity back. Through the death and resurrection of Jesus Christ, the ideological powers of this world are deconstructed and defeated, revealing the possibility of a new way of life in the world grounded in grace and love.

Capitalism, as an ideology, is not the only way to engage with the economic sphere that is essential to social life. A meaningful critique of capitalism includes asking important questions about the nature of economic life and how it might contribute to human flourishing. Youth ministry must recognize how the capitalist ideology shapes the lives of young people and invite them to reclaim economic life in a way that is grounded in the gospel. This is not an application of Christian morality or a connection of Christian jargon to current economic processes; it must instead be a reexamination of the processes themselves through the deconstruction of dehumanizing forms of ideology in order to live into humanizing forms of economic life together.

Taking Youth Ministry to the Desert

The Desert Fathers and Mothers were a group of Christians who, in the third and fourth centuries, went out to the desert to encounter God and live spiritual lives. The most famous is Saint Anthony, who—upon hearing the Gospel reading in which Jesus tells the rich, young ruler that if he wants to be perfect, he should sell his possessions and give the money to the poor—divested himself of his wealth, entrusted his younger sister to a group of nuns, and went into the desert.

The desert became a place where early Christians could practice an alternative way of life in obedience to God. As Christianity became the accepted religion of the empire, desert monasticism became a new form of martyrdom in which people "died" to their inwardly turned, sinful lives so they might be reborn into a new humanity revealed in Jesus Christ. But it was more than that. Desert spirituality takes seriously the power of cultural ideology. When you believe the social and cultural forces that shape identity and social life are badly twisted and deformed, you go to a place where you can create something new. Like the Israelites being led out of Egypt and into the desert, the place where God purges them of their Egyptian ways, the Desert Fathers and Mothers went to the desert to be purged of their old ways of life.

There are stereotypes and misconceptions associated with desert monasticism, especially within the Protestant tradition. Some see it as rejecting the call of Jesus to preach the good news to the world—How can you evangelize when you live in the desert? Others see it as a refusal to love our neighbor. A more serious engagement of the Desert Fathers and Mothers recognizes how desert life is not a rejection of this world but a confrontation of cultural ideology. In this way, desert life is iconoclastic, as it breaks open accepted ways of life to examine the underlying formative power at work.[1] The purpose of going out to the desert is to establish an alternative society shaped by a different set of social values. Scholar John Chryssavgis describes it this way: "Society expects its citizens to be active and productive. In society, you are useless if you are not valuable. . . . The desert fathers and mothers proclaimed a different set of values, where change occurs through silence and not war; where inaction may be the most powerful source of action; and where productivity may be measured by obscurity, even invisibility."[2] Rather than holding contempt for humanity, the way of the desert seeks to explore the depths of what it means to be human by ridding ourselves of the ideological distortions we unknowingly accept.

The desert, in this context, is a place of revolution and transfiguration.[3] It's an experience through which we come to discover and embrace our deeper emotions and motivations as we become conscious of our desires and aware of our weaknesses. The desert life insists that there's no way around this struggle to become more aware of our human selves—it's a struggle that can only be embraced and gone through. This is why temptation is at the heart of the desert experience, because our sinful nature longs to transcend our human limitations and avoid the reality of our finite humanity. The proper response is not flight, it's "hard labor and patience."[4]

The Desert Monastics see the restless movement from place to place, the inability to commit to a place or community, as the real temptation. This manifests itself in the refusal to listen, wait, or watch. The desert life, by contrast, is a commitment to a place through suffering or hardship. This commitment prepares people for life together and serves as a building block for social life. The detachment of the desert is not about annihilation; it's about freedom—the freedom to focus on all things without being consumed by anything. It's about learning to live in the world with open hands instead of clenched fists. It's about shedding the excess layers and learning to live with less. Finally, it's about recognizing the presence of God in the midst of the struggle, not at the end. Human life is not something to be overcome to get to some eternal heaven where we can finally be with God. In Jesus Christ, we recognize the presence of God in the midst of this life, in the midst of our suffering and hardship, in a way that affirms this finite, temporal life is good.

Joan Chittister's *In God's Holy Light: Wisdom from the Desert Monastics* tells the story of two desert monks—Abba Daniel and Abba Ammoes. Abba Ammoes, the younger monk, sees life as compartmentalized. God is found in the monastery, in the cell, while those outside are enemies. Abba Daniel, however, corrects him: "Who shall separate us henceforth from God? God is in the cell, and, on the other hand, He is outside too."[5] For Abba Daniel, human life cannot be easily separated into the religious and the secular; all of life is a "word of God, teaching him something, requiring something from him in return."[6] Chittister writes, "Abba Daniel, wise old monk, knows that the purpose of the spiritual life is not to separate us from others. On the contrary, it is meant to unite us, but all too often is it used to divide us."[7] She goes on to say, "We are meant to identify with the hopes and fears, and the needs and struggles, of the whole world—because the world is God's, and we are God's agents on earth."[8]

Understanding the wholeness of human life before God prevents us from relegating the economic sphere to the secular as something separate from faith. Economic life is an integral part of social life in which humans work to meet individual and communal needs—the Desert Fathers and Mothers understood this. Seeing economic life as an integral part of faith and spirituality means asking deep questions about how the death and resurrection of Jesus Christ open up a new way of being human in the world. In a similar way, the Christian community should invite young people to see economic life as a word God speaks to us by inviting them out from the distortions of economic life that misshape our identities and into new practices that seek the flourishing of all of creation.

Even though the Desert Fathers and Mothers lived almost two thousand years ago, they addressed economic issues that speak to our contemporary experience. Chittister tells this story: "Abban

Evagrius said that there was a brother, called Serapion, who didn't own anything except the Gospel, and this he sold to feed the poor. And he said these words, which are worth remembering: 'I have even sold the very word which commanded me: "Sell everything and give to the poor."'"[9] Chittister sees in this story an application to our contemporary society: "Here in this simple story we are confronted in the starkest terms with what centuries later is still a very modern attachment. Private ownership, the tendency to amass wealth, is in our time the very foundation of globalism, the sure sign of social success, and the system on which all private security depends in a capitalist world."[10] What we are willing to give away raises important questions for our capitalist economic system, a system that is predicated on self-interest. Yet the gospel presents an understanding of the human self that is open to God and the world. Through the death and resurrection of Christ, we experience the death of our inwardly turned sinful self, giving way to the resurrection life that moves outward toward God and neighbor.

The importance of work is also found in the desert. Work has always been central to monastic life, along with prayer and solitude, as a way to benefit the community. Chittister summarizes this by saying, "And yet, in a culture of Desert Monastics, all of whom live highly individualized spiritual lives, the basis of community . . . is exactly the opposite. The monastic says, 'I have never wanted work that was useful to me but loss to my brother.' Today, the question of who or what will be hurt by the work I'm doing is yet to be part of the social conscience."[11] She goes on to say, "The wisdom of the Desert Monastics about work is clearer in this century than it might have even been in their own time. It is time to prove to ourselves and others that the way we earn our own living is life-enhancing for others as well. 'I never wanted work that was useful to me but loss to my brother,' the old man says. Yet before that can ever be the situation again, we are all going to need to understand why we were created in the first place."[12]

The Desert Fathers and Mothers show a focused attempt to undo every cultural ideology that distorts our humanity by causing hatred and violence. Going to the desert was an act of death—like the Israelites going through the wilderness and Jesus going to the cross. However, the biblical pattern is to move through death to new life. The Desert Monastics sought to die to their sinful selves, to be stripped of every false understanding so they might be given new life—so they could see clearly. My students react negatively to the desert life. They claim to value community and want to make a difference in the world. To this I respond, What if our sense of community isn't community at all? What if what we think is community is an inwardly turned distortion that keeps us from loving God and our neighbor? Maybe we need to learn from the Desert Fathers and Mothers so we can have our eyes and ears opened. Maybe the way of the desert—the way of death and resurrection—is the way to true community, true life, and true humanity.

Rowan Williams and Human Consciousness

When I ask young people what it means to be human, I get a range of answers, from "created in the image of God" to "we have souls" to an emphasis on rationality and morality. Each of these answers simply raises more questions about what the Bible means when it says humans are created in the image of God—questions about the relationship between our bodies and our souls or how fields like neuroscience have opened up new ways of thinking about human consciousness.

The issue of consciousness is central to the conversation about what it means to be human. There is much discussion and debate about what can be known about consciousness and whether it is grounded in material processes of the brain or something else.[13] In *Being Human: Bodies, Minds, Persons*, theologian and philosopher Rowan Williams suggests that consciousness represents a point of view—the vantage point from which we "bump into things."[14] This point of view constitutes the unified "I" with which humans make meaning of the world through language.[15] Human consciousness is the vantage point from which we encounter the world, an encounter that is mediated through our senses and given meaning through language. As we bump into objects in the world, we use symbols—sounds, letters, words—to narrate our experiences and situate ourselves.

When I am in the front yard playing catch with my ten-year-old neighbor, I do this as a conscious human being fully aware of the meaningful activity I am engaged in. Language is what provides meaning as I use my glove, throw a baseball, and talk about the types of pitches I'm about to throw. This encounter is meaningful because of the signs—the green grass, the warm air, the blue sky, the ball and glove, and the other conscious human being with whom I am playing catch. Human consciousness is the organizing force that takes these multiple experiences and makes meaning. At the heart of the ability to make meaning, for Williams, is relationality. He writes, "Consciousness as we normally think about it has a relational dimension. I can't think without thinking of the other. I can't even think of my body, this zero point of orientation, without understanding that it's an object to another. I am seen, I am heard, I am understood. . . . To have a point of view is to understand that the world is constructed out of diverse points of orientation."[16] While he goes on to talk about narrative, time, and language, for our purposes it's enough to say that human identity is fundamentally relational; it is to exist within a network of relational coordinates that give meaning. Williams writes, "What makes me a person, and what makes me this person rather than another, is not simply a set of facts. . . . I stand in the middle of a network of relations, the point where the lines cross."[17]

This understanding of the human person as a network of relationships is supported by Scripture. While the image of God for humanity in the opening chapter of Genesis is found in the way humans represent God within the creation, in Genesis 2, human creatures are defined by their relationships. Genesis 2:7 says, "Then the Lord God formed a man from the dust of the ground and breathed into his nostrils the breath of life, and the man became a living being." Here, the human person is created from the ground; we are part of this created world and deeply connected with all of creation. Forgetting this connection alienates us from the foundation of embodied existence. We are made from the dust of the earth, but we have been made alive by the very breath of God. Thus, we are never just dust; to be a human person is to be alive with the breath or spirit of God. These two relationships—our connection with the material creation and the life-giving spirit of God—are the basis of our human life. Verse 18 reads, "It is not good that the man should be alone; I will make him a helper as his partner" (NRSVUE). This leads to the creation of the woman from the rib and Adam's hymn of praise when he first sees Eve: "This at last is bone of my bones and flesh of my flesh; this one shall be called Woman, for out of Man this one was taken" (v. 23 NRSVUE). Thus, to be a human person is to live with others, to have our identities given to us not just by God but by those with whom we live in community. The chapter ends with a declaration of wholeness: "And the man and his wife were both naked and were not ashamed" (v. 25 NRSVUE). Being human beings, according to Genesis 2, means that our lives come from outside of ourselves—in relationship with God, creation, and others.

All of this is undone by human sin in Genesis 3. After they eat of the tree, they hide from God (Gen 3:8). Instead of a hymn of praise, the man now blames the woman for everything that has happened (Gen 3:12). The woman blames the serpent, which leads to a curse on the ground, shattering the relationship between humanity and creation. Sin leads to a fracturing of life-giving relationships, leading to an inwardly turned existence alienated from God and our neighbor. Sin cuts through every part of our existence, including our economic relationships. Our tendency is to be inwardly turned, to see creation and our neighbor as having commodities to be owned and manipulated for our own gain. Our tendency is to want to overcome our embodied, creaturely life, no longer seeking wholeness and flourishing but always seeking progress and abstraction.

Yet the biblical story shows how God continuously searches for us. Like God searching for the man and woman in the garden, God comes to Abraham and makes a covenant—establishing a relational commitment that reverberates throughout the Old Testament and the story of the people of Israel: "You will be my people, and I will be your God" (Jer 30:22). But this vertical relationship has a horizontal dimension, fulfilled in the command to love God and love our neighbor. Throughout the Torah, God's law for the people of Israel, the culturally conditioned codes reveal the truth about human identity—that we are to care for the poor, the widow, or the orphan by leaving part of the crop in the field for them to glean, that we are to treat the foreigner in our midst well, like we would treat our own citizens. We are to be careful with how we lend and borrow money, making sure we don't cause people to end up in crushing forms of debt or poverty. (See Lev 19 and Deut 14–15.)

All of this is fulfilled in the person of Jesus Christ, who is the full expression of God's love for humanity and for this world. In Jesus Christ, we see the covenant between humanity and God fulfilled, as Christ is fully human and fully divine, the embodiment of God's presence in and with humanity. By faith, we are invited to live as the new humanity of Jesus Christ in the world, bearing witness to what it means to be a human person, loving God and loving neighbor.

What This Means for Youth Ministry

The task of youth ministry is to cultivate a form of Christian spirituality that is fundamentally about living as a human person in right relationship with God and with our neighbor. To be a human creature, as Williams points out, is to exist as an embodied consciousness through which one encounters the outside world. Thus, a truly Christian perspective of what it means to be a human person is that we exist as ensouled bodies. Our humanity is not the abstract soul trapped in a human body, nor is it just material stuff. Holding the proper tension is crucial to embracing our identity as human creatures made in the image of God.

As stated earlier, youth ministry has the tendency to foster a dualistic approach to human identity and Christian faith. While most youth pastors would agree that to be human is to live an embodied life, in practice, evangelical youth ministry doesn't hold this tension well. The focus tends toward a view of the gospel that focuses on otherworldly salvation that comes from accepting Jesus into our hearts. Issues relating to our embodied lives are addressed in a way that treats them as symptoms. Sexuality, substance abuse, bullying, mental health, justice, and so on are increasingly topics for discussion within youth ministry. The tendency, however, is to see them as problems that are resolved by faith in Jesus. Faith in Jesus provides comfort, courage, and hope for young people as they deal with these issues in their personal lives.

Cultivating a faith in Jesus Christ, however it might be expressed, is an important part of youth ministry. So too is providing young people with the assurance that faith can give comfort in difficult times. However, these issues are often not dealt with from a holistic perspective. Just as youth ministry should help disciple young people into relationships with Jesus, it also needs to help them understand how discipleship calls them into a new way of being human in the world. The call to follow Christ is not a call out of this world; it is a call back into the world for the sake of the world. Christians are called to a new way of life within their networks of relationships. Christ doesn't call us out of our creaturely existence; Christ picks us up, gives us the new breath of the Holy Spirit in our lungs, and reconnects us to the life-giving relationships that make us human beings. Then Christ sends us back into the world to live as members of the body (the new humanity) of the resurrected Christ.

Andrew Root's interpretation of faith and spirituality in the "secular age" insightfully shows us how within the immanent frame of secularity, politics, science, technology, and economics are the dominant forces governing our lives. One response is to fight against these secular worldviews by trying to return to an older understanding of transcendence. An example is how adults complain about how young people are too connected to their phones, too busy with sports or jobs, or too consumeristic. While there may be a kernel of truth to this, there's a better way to respond. Instead, the Christian community should help young people engage with these spheres of creaturely life from the vantage point of Christian faith so they might recognize how they are part of the relational networks that make us human persons. The proper response, in the context of the secular age, is for youth ministry to see its mission as the engagement of these cultural spheres in a way that allows young people to cultivate biblical and theological wisdom.

Understanding the relational dimension of human identity provides an important entry point into a discussion of economic life. Because economics is about how human persons meet basic (and not-so-basic) needs, it focuses on networks of relationships, institutions, and structures that make this type of engagement easier for some and more difficult for others. Again, whether young people are aware of this or not, they—like the rest of us—are caught up in systems of production, exchange, and consumption that shape our identities by shaping our views of the world. Just as sin cuts through every human person, tempting them to live inwardly turned lives, so too does sin cut through the economic sphere, producing forms of ideology that distort our economic relationships. Social entrepreneurship—the use of business practices to bring social transformation and challenge the ideological forces at work in economics—can raise awareness of the hidden ideological impulses of these systems and networks that produce inequality and get in the way of human flourishing. Thus, it has the potential to be a valuable tool for the Christian community and youth ministry to help young people develop a deeper understanding of this sphere of human life. More than that, it provides a way for youth ministry to challenge the social and cultural ideological forces that misdirect and distort our economic relationships. Rather than dealing with the symptoms that stem from the capitalist abstraction of human identity, social entrepreneurship provides a way to unmask it and equip young people to participate in economic life in a way that seeks flourishing and justice. It also provides youth ministry with a tool to help cultivate the courage and hope that come with skills grounded in wisdom, opening them up to possibilities they never would or could have imagined.

The sort of economy we want—or to put it differently, how we help direct economic activity toward the flourishing of our neighbor, our community, and the world—is a question for youth ministry. Youth leaders must help young people connect the economic aspect of their human identity with their Christian faith. What better place than youth ministry to help them wrestle with what the gospel means for their work, their consumption, and the way they meet their basic needs? Within this context, we can help them see the connections between economics and justice by looking at how God has equipped us to seek the flourishing of our neighbor.

Ultimately, a youth ministry / social entrepreneurship partnership can help young people move outward from the church into the community. It can allow them to recognize the needs of the community and equip them with the insight to meet these through economic development—the integration of faith and business in a way that seeks human flourishing and justice grounded in the death and resurrection of Jesus.

Four

Seeking the Welfare of the City

Jason Lief

A few years ago, I went with our church's youth group on a trip to Chicago. This wasn't a typical mission trip—we didn't do much work. We served lunch in a soup kitchen one afternoon; otherwise, most of our time was spent immersed in the neighborhoods of Chicago. One day, we drove from neighborhood to neighborhood to learn about street art. We visited cultural centers and businesses and explored different communities. We discussed the political, social, and economic challenges facing many people living in the city. But these issues were always framed within a conversation about the resources already available to the people and institutions within each community. The point wasn't for us white people from rural Iowa to "serve"—meaning "save"—the people living in the city by painting their houses and giving them Jesus; the point was to go see and hear how God was already at work in the people living in the community.

One morning, we visited a coffee shop called Kusanya, a Swahili word that means "to gather," located in the Englewood neighborhood. The shop was opened by Phil Sipka, a Fuller Seminary graduate, and some neighbors in the area to provide a gathering space for the neighborhood. A newspaper article about the coffee shop described it as follows:

> When Phil Sipka and some of his Englewood neighbors opened a cafe a year ago this week, skeptics had suggestions. How about rolling security gates over the wall-size windows? Or a permanently locked door, with a buzzer to buzz customers in? Maybe a nighttime security guard. Sipka and his neighbors had a different idea. "Let's be vulnerable," he said Thursday, sitting at one of the tables he made from reclaimed wood. "I think people respect intentional vulnerability."
>
> The cafe is named Kusanya, a Swahili word that means "to gather," and though it's in a neighborhood that makes news most often when someone makes trouble, it has managed to stay safe since it opened last Nov. 19. No bricks or bullets have come through its windows. No thieves have breached the doors. The cafe has cultivated a loyal clientele, which on Thursday included Aaron Walker and several other Streets & Sanitation workers who collect garbage nearby. "This is like an oasis in the desert," Walker said. He was eating a chicken funKadelic sandwich ($4.81), which rivals the Tuna Turner ($4.81) as his favorite menu item. "I love the ambience," he said. "The food is good. I love the coffee. This beats McDonald's fried this and grease that."
>
> Kusanya, which is run as a nonprofit, occupies a century-old building on West 69th Street that once housed Dot's Lounge. Sipka and his allies spent several years looking for a location, stymied by all the things that work against businesses. . . . Englewood building owners, Sipka said, often live outside the neighborhood and aren't eager to make improvements. Banks aren't eager to make loans. Vacant lots abound. And of all the things the neighborhood needs, a cafe might seem low on the list. Sipka, however,

believes that a safe, intimate, attractive place for neighbors to sit down together, with good food and good coffee, can breed bigger changes. Can. May. It's still an experiment. "The hard part about our vision is that we can't control it," he said. "We can't force empowerment. We can just create the opportunity."[1]

By providing good coffee, quality food, and a place for people in the community to gather, Kusanya represents a force of change and transformation as young people learn the skills of being a barista as well as how to roast their own coffee. It is a gathering space for artists, musicians, and anyone else who has a cultural activity to share. Kusanya is an example of what it looks like to think outside the box, to cultivate a vision for a space and place that many cannot or will not see. It shows how a business can be used to promote human flourishing by challenging the accepted paradigm of the status quo and enacting change.

Let's Get Practical

Youth ministry is a form of practical theology. This doesn't mean practical versus impractical—it means theory versus action. Theological beliefs (theory) are deeply connected to ways of life (action). Understanding this connection provides a framework for differentiating between espoused and operational theological beliefs. Espoused beliefs are the official teachings, doctrines, or principles a person or community claims to uphold—for example, the belief that all people are made in the image of God and worthy of love and respect. Most Christians, if asked if they believe this, will wholeheartedly agree because this is what their church teaches. These same people can turn around and engage in actions or with systems that either explicitly or implicitly foster racism and discrimination. Some might say this is because we are all sinful and fall short (another espoused belief), but often there's more going on. Most behavior is not shaped by rational beliefs—what are called the executive functions of the mind. Instead, our behavior is influenced by the ingrained habits that unconsciously shape behavior and thus shape identity. These habits are informed by the operational beliefs that unconsciously inform the way individuals and communities view the world.

This is a fundamental problem with youth ministry: youth leaders teach young people what to believe about God and living a moral life, assuming these ideas will lead to transformation, but these doctrinal or moral lessons rarely address the ingrained ideological habits formed by the dominant culture. This kind of instruction creates a disconnect between the teachings of the church (espoused beliefs) and the way young people live (operational beliefs). Treating youth ministry as a form of practical theology works to uncover these operational beliefs.

The mission trip to Chicago shows the difference between espoused and operational beliefs. My youth group could have spent time talking about poverty, racism, and what the Bible says about these issues. We could have focused on more stereotypical mission trip activities, serving in various ways but also trying to convert people and tell them about Jesus. Instead, I immersed my young people in the diversity of Chicago. My youth group experienced this coffee shop that represents a creative attempt by the community to foster change through praxis (action) rather than making sure people have the right ideas or principles. All praxis and all our behaviors are embedded with ideas. The academic term for this is *theory-laden praxis*—the recognition that our actions are deeply intertwined with ideas, both conscious and subconscious. It's never an either/or choice between action or ideas. Rather, practical theology means starting with action, or with what's happening, then working to uncover both operational and espoused beliefs to try to determine why they might be different and how to enact change.

Youth ministry as practical theology is interdisciplinary. Youth ministry is not only about theology, the Bible, or doctrine; it is also about bringing theology into conversation with other disciplines. Often, these conversations include psychology or sociology for those doing pastoral care. However, in this instance, we're suggesting the fields of business and economics. I can hear the objection: I'm a youth pastor, not a businessperson. Fair enough. This is why the integration of social entrepreneurship with youth ministry must be a community project. The youth pastor can't be a lone ranger; they must be a facilitator, inviting other members of the congregation with expertise in the areas of business and economics to help provide insight and leadership.

Framing youth ministry within practical theology requires the task of ministry to always be involved with a particular theological method. Leaders must engage in this work from a particular paradigm or approach. There are multiple approaches to choose from, depending on one's philosophical and theological commitments.

Understanding the relationship between theory and practice is essential within pastoral ministry. This means taking seriously the relationship between belief and action. In her book *Transforming Practice*, Elaine Graham addresses this by claiming that "theory and practice do not exist independently. . . . Christian praxis—value-directed and value-laden action—is understood as the medium through which the Christian community embodies and enacts its fundamental vision of the Gospel."[2] Thus, discipleship involves taking the time to recognize the implicit operational beliefs that inform practices many in the Christian community take for granted. This means that theology is never a set of abstract ideas; it is a way of life in which beliefs about God and the world are lived within a particular context. For Graham, this means the focus of theological reflection must be understood as "orthopraxis, or authentic transformatory action, rather than orthodoxy (right belief)." [3]

Graham takes a middle position between abstract ideas and lived experience. On the one hand, there are those who believe that if people have the right ideas, they will go out into the world and enact those ideas. On the other side, there are those who believe concrete action is where everything starts. Graham shows how ideas and action are intertwined and that every action or practice has theory, or ideas, embedded within it. We may not be aware of how these ideas shape how we're acting, but this doesn't detract from their power to inform our actions.

Take shooting a basketball. In practice, coaches have players go through drills that form how they shoot the ball. Coaches could sit players down and tell them the theory that informs the practice, or they could just roll the ball out and tell them to shoot with no instruction. Instead, they use drills (practice) to develop their shooting abilities. These drills are infused with theory, even if coaches and players are unaware of it. Graham applies this idea to the church. According to Graham, giving people abstract doctrinal knowledge doesn't produce transformation. Neither does going out into the world to share the love of Jesus. What brings transformation is cultivating a different way of life informed by the revelation of God's love for the world in Jesus Christ. This third way is the recognition that theological knowledge must be grounded in a way of life.

Graham provides a way to reflect on the economic praxis of the broader culture and the impact it has on communities. From this perspective, capitalism is not a neutral approach to economic life any more than socialism is. The economic practices of capitalism are infused with theory—a particular interpretation of what it means to be human and of the purpose and goal of economic activity. This ideology permeates the cultural world of young people, shaping how they see the world. A Christian approach to economic life is what Kathryn Tanner explores by asking questions about an economy of grace. This approach informs the economic practices of the Desert Fathers and Mothers as they seek to faithfully love God and their neighbor in their economic relationships. Social entrepreneurship and youth ministry can have profound impacts on the lives of young people by inviting them into a new approach to economic life infused with the biblical and theological revelation of what it means to be human. Through this approach, young people are invited into a holistic discipleship in which they wrestle with what it means to love God and their neighbor in the economic sphere of life. They are confronted with challenges of discipleship as they work out their faith with, as Paul says, "fear and trembling." In this context, Scripture, theology, and the Christian tradition are all contextualized as young people are confronted with the question, What does it mean to live in this world—and love this world—as the new people of God in Jesus Christ?

For youth ministry to engage the lived experience of young people, it must take seriously the practice of theological interpretation. Because this includes paying attention to the implicit beliefs that inform our way of life, it is helpful to see this as a process of cultural interpretation. In the book *Introduction to Practical Theology*, Richard Osmer provides useful steps for individuals and communities to engage in this process. For Osmer, practical theological interpretation takes place in four tasks:

1. **Descriptive-empirical:** "Gathering information that helps us discern patterns and dynamics in particular episodes, situations, or contexts."[4] The first task begins with practice by asking the fundamental question, "What is going on?"

This involves an assessment of needs—both the needs of the young people who are part of a church's community as well as the needs of the broader community. For example, in my community, the pandemic revealed a need for a diaper bank. While many organizations were addressing issues related to food, health care, and other basic needs, there was a gap in providing young mothers and families with diapers and other necessities to care for their children. The easy thing is to start with ideas: our church should help people during this pandemic. From there, it's easy to fall into the patterns of donating money, starting a food drive, and so on. While these things are all good in and of themselves, they are examples of answering a question that isn't being asked. These needs were already being met by organizations in the community. By taking the time to figure out what was happening and what the true needs were, my church was able to focus its attention on meeting the needs of mothers, children, and families. Other communities may not need a diaper bank or a coffee shop, but there may be different needs to uncover. This first step in assessing what's going on is to do an analysis of the needs of the community by reaching out to local organizations and leaders.

2. **Interpretive task:** "Drawing on theories of the arts and sciences to better understand and explain why these patterns and dynamics are occurring."[5] The question at the heart of this task is, "Why is this going on?" Pastoral care and youth ministry are about interpretation. We interpret the words people say, their body language, the stories they tell, and even their presence and absence. To care for young people well is to pay attention to how they articulate their identities and the contextual issues that shape how they see the world.

This also means interpreting what's happening in the broader community and helping them understand the social and cultural forces at work in the lives of their neighbors. An important part of this step is trying to understand the gap that can exist between espoused and operational beliefs. When it comes to a diaper bank, helping young people understand the economic and social realities of many young families and single parents opens them up to a better understanding of the need for it. In my community, the need for a diaper bank pushes into the issue of immigration, as there are many undocumented immigrants working in our agricultural community. Seeing the issue of diapers within this broader context helps young people better understand the needs of their neighbors and the complex issues that are at work.

3. **Normative task:** "Using theological concepts to interpret particular episodes, situations, or contexts, constructing ethical norms to guide our responses, and learning from 'good practice.'"[6] The question that guides this task is, "What ought to be going on?" *Ought* is a loaded word; it can imply some sort of abstract norm that must be enforced. Here, it means more about what flourishing looks like in the context of the gospel. The youth pastor, using biblical and theological perspectives in dialogue with other disciplines, helps young people read and understand Scripture. We help them understand theological beliefs within the context of their lived experience. As youth leaders uncover young people's operational beliefs and help them become aware of them, we can bring them into conversation with the message of the gospel. The same understanding is true of the broader community. The interpretive process leads to the question of flourishing: How do we best help people

take care of their children in healthy ways? Diapers are about the health of the child and the family. The diaper bank is grounded in the normative task, which asked how my church might help people take care of their kids. Embedded in this are the biblical and theological perspectives that call us to love God and love our neighbors, care for immigrants and the poor, and seek justice and mercy. This involves ethical concerns that include economics, politics, biology, and environmental science. All of this provides the foundation for the final task.

4. **Pragmatic task:** "Determining strategies of action that will influence situations in ways that are desirable and entering into reflective conversation with the talk back emerging when they are enacted."[7] The youth pastor and those they lead develop a course of action that addresses what is actually happening. Another way to see it is the youth pastor or leader addresses uncovered operational beliefs and the questions or issues young people are grappling with. Too often, youth leaders fail to recognize that young people give us what they think we want to hear. Our task is to try to uncover what's really happening. The other tasks provide the basis for new actions that bring theological reflection to bear on concrete situations. Regarding the diaper bank, this involves research, planning, meetings, financing, presentations—the nuts and bolts of starting up a nonprofit.

Osmer and Graham offer an important theological framework for the spiritual formation and pastoral care of young people by focusing on lived experience. Too often, practice and theory are set against each other, with one side emphasizing action, while the other focuses on right beliefs. Graham and Osmer show that this is a false choice. The faith formation of young people happens when biblical and theological insights are connected to their lived experience, including the concrete needs of their neighbors. This approach allows youth pastors to focus care not on some abstract ideal they want every young person to attain but on the material reality in which they live. It also allows them to cultivate the humanity of young people by encouraging their unique gifts, which young people often see as disconnected from faith. There are many young people who don't fit in within a youth group or community because they have different interests. This approach allows a youth leader to find ways to put these gifts and talents to work.

A few years back, in my life as a high school teacher, one of my responsibilities was to organize the service day—a day when students would go out into the community and work. I separated the students into groups that were each led by a teacher. After the groups had been posted, a teacher came up to me and said sarcastically, "Thanks a lot!" A certain junior student, who was difficult to have in class, was in his group. Knowing he was a serial school skipper, I responded, "Well, maybe he won't come?" Service day came, and he showed up. When the day was over and groups were coming back to campus, I ran into the teacher and asked him how it went. "You wouldn't believe it," he said. Apparently, this young person, though not a stellar student, was gifted at landscaping. Not only was he the best worker of the group, but my colleague gushed about the wonderful conversations they had as they worked together the entire day. In school, this young man was difficult and seen as a troublemaker. However, when given the opportunity to put his gifts to use, he demonstrated another side. This is the power and potential of bringing social entrepreneurship into youth ministry—it provides one more way for young people to connect and find meaning.

Making the Connection: Social Entrepreneurship and Practical Theology

Similar to practical theology, the transformative power of social entrepreneurship involves an act of interpretation. In *Getting beyond Better: How Social Entrepreneurship Works*, Roger Martin and Sally Osberg describe this interpretive action in four stages:

1. **Understanding the world:** "The paradox of social transformation is that one has to truly understand the system as it is before any serious attempt can be made to change it."
2. **Envisioning a new future:** "To make a positive difference, every change agent, whether social entrepreneur or not, needs to set a direction."
3. **Building a model for change:** "To bring a vision to life, social entrepreneurs must apply creativity and resourcefulness to building a model for change—one that is sustainable in that it reduces costs or increases value in a systemic and permanent way that can be quantified and captured."
4. **Scaling the solution:** "Models that require constant reapplication of the same level of investment regardless of scale will commonly fail to produce sustainable equilibrium change."[8]

The connection between these four stages and Osmer's four tasks of practical theology is that both try to understand what's happening within a community in a way that makes change possible. Understanding the world involves deciphering the difference between espoused and operational principles. It means working to unmask unspoken ideological paradigms to foster change. True transformation is grounded in the possibility that things can be different, that there's an alternative narrative than the one in operation—in other words, it's being able to envision a new future. The eschato-logical impulses of practical theology and social entrepreneurship are reflected in a belief that the patterns of this world are not fixed. The possibility for change becomes a reality by marshaling the theologi-cal and social resources needed to build something new, challenging and changing old patterns, and opening individuals and communities to a new way of life. All of this, of course, must be sustainable and scaled in such a way that it can carry on, becoming a catalyst for change and transformation grounded in the gospel.

Transformation takes place at multiple levels. First, the youth are transformed as they come to see the gospel connected to their lived experience. Bringing social entrepreneurship together with youth ministry helps them see how biblical and theological reflec-tion are deeply connected with a way of life in this world. Biblical and theological teaching become less about abstract spirituality or moral principles and more about what it means to live into the new human-ity of Jesus Christ in this world. This means helping young people envision the kingdom of God as a new way of life made possible by the death and resurrection of Jesus Christ. Our job as youth leaders is to provide a context in which young people can see and experience this reality.

Second, this approach transforms the way young people approach the idea of a calling or vocation. Currently, many Chris-tians approach the idea of a calling in a dualistic way. We feel God calling us to business or education, and we understand our roles within these fields in a moral or evangelistic way, while the struc-ture and practices of these fields are left to function according to their own ideological principles. Bringing social entrepreneurship and youth ministry together means helping young people recognize the goodness of these different fields, specifically business and eco-nomics. They are part of God's good creation, and while they have become distorted by sin, they are reconciled in Christ. As Paul writes in Colossians, "For in him all the fullness of God was pleased to dwell, and through him God was pleased to reconcile to himself all things, whether on earth or in heaven, by making peace through the blood of his cross" (1:19–20 NRSVUE). As a Christian, my calling is more than being moral in an unjust system; it is to be a sign of God's new creation and transformation within unjust systems by helping nurture the flourishing of all creation.

Embracing Secularity

There is an expression of secularity that is good. At the heart of the Christian faith is the belief that there is one God revealed in three persons. All other powers that claim to be gods are imposters. Today, most people in the West do not encounter false gods in the sense of idols or other deities. Nonetheless, idolatry remains a pervasive part of our experience. John Calvin claimed that the human heart is an idol factory. Karl Barth famously opposed natural theology, the belief that we can know God through creation, because of his experience with the idolatry of Nazi Germany. He insisted that natural theology always leads to idolatry, something he based on Romans 1. More significantly, Paul's declaration that our struggle is not against flesh and blood but against the principles and powers of the present age helps make my point that secularity is a good thing. What happens with the rise of the secular age is that the world is, as Bonhoeffer said, "free to be the world." Our cultural and social patterns, the ideological beliefs that support those patterns, and our political and economic theories all take on lives of their own—they become powers that cease to be good and become idols.

The twentieth-century French author Jacques Ellul focused on technology and the way it dominates our lives. Though he's often misread as a Luddite, it's important to recognize what Ellul actually opposes: oppressive ideology in all its forms. In his book *The Meaning of the City*, Ellul talks about the ways in which the cultural and technological patterns begin to take on lives of their own.[9] They become "deified," seen as the ultimate sources of meaning and life even as they dehumanize and enslave. For Ellul, the cross and resurrection are the means by which God disrupts and defeats these powers. In doing so, they cease to be gods, and they are free to be used again as tools. Jesus refers to money as *mammon*—a power that corrupts and dominates. This continues to be the story of money in our own day. More than anything else in Western culture, money serves as the source of meaning and identity, dominating every area of life. On the cross, Jesus defeats mammon, making it possible for us to use money not as a god or as the all-powerful source of meaning but as a tool—a means of exchange. In social entrepreneurship as we have discussed it here, economic practices and resources are tools to be used for the sake of human flourishing and justice.

Bringing youth ministry and social entrepreneurship together opens the possibility of helping young people see how money can distort our humanity when it becomes an idol supported by ideology, but it also can help them see how the economic sphere of life is a part of creation that can be used to seek flourishing and justice in the world. Youth pastors can show young people how to cultivate and create an economy of grace, one that doesn't reduce people to their economic value but utilizes economic relationships to help others flourish. Bringing social entrepreneurship together with youth ministry provides an opportunity for the church to transform the way young people see their communities, their relationships, their institutions, and even their careers. By utilizing the biblical and theological language of the Christian tradition, we can help young people discover identity and meaning in ways that recognize how the kingdom of God is breaking into and transforming this world.

Back to Chicago

One afternoon, we took our group to an urban farm developed on the land where the Robert Taylor housing complex, one of the more notorious public housing failures in Chicago, once stood. We went there to learn about the program and help with some work. Many of the young people jumped right in—weeding, harvesting, laying dirt, laying watering strips, and helping in other ways. Because they're from rural Iowa, they already had the skills and knowledge to do the work. Interestingly, farming is something many of them take for granted. It's a way of life. In Chicago, they were given the opportunity to see how their knowledge and skills could be used to bring about social transformation. That night, as we debriefed, I could see and hear the wheels turning. The students didn't know, they had never imagined, that farming could bring about social and economic transformation. Taking for granted the availability of fresh food at reasonable costs, they had never thought about "food deserts" in urban areas or how city planning can make or break the health and well-being of people living in a particular neighborhood. Our church failed to help our young people imagine how their gardening or farming skills might be utilized to bring about transformation in Iowa. We had never encouraged them to think about how tilling the soil connects with loving God and loving our neighbor. We had to go to Chicago to hear this good news.

Bringing youth ministry together with social entrepreneurship offers a lesson in eschatology—a fancy way of talking about hope. The world as it presently exists is not the final word about the way things are or will be. The resurrection of Jesus and the pouring out of the Holy Spirit at Pentecost remind us that God is always making this world new. History bends not only toward justice but toward hope, toward newness, toward flourishing. Young people need to hear and embody this message by putting their talents to work. The task of youth ministry is to spark the imaginations of young people so they can see beyond the way things presently are to the way God is transforming them to be in Jesus Christ—for their sake and for the sake of the world.

Five

Going Off Script with God's Mission

Kurt Rietema

From the outside looking in, this wasn't anyone's A-team. To be honest, the kids who were a part of our first attempt at ImagineX, the youth social entrepreneurship program I've led with a few friends for the last seven years, were just my neighbors' kids who didn't have anything better to do in the summer. What's more, they were most likely cajoled by their parents to get out of the house and hang out with me because they pitied me. The group and I live in a place called Argentine, a working-class neighborhood of Kansas City, Kansas, with a rich Latino culture mashed up with banal, 1970s public housing projects where recently arrived refugees with hearts still drunk on the promise of the American dream share too-thin walls with others who grew up in generational poverty and laugh at their new neighbors' naivete. The team of young people reflected all of that beautiful complexity.

There was a brother and sister from the Congo who barely spoke English. Then there was Zaira across the street, who carried not only the weight of her parents' immigration status but also that of their expectations. Rhiannon lived next door to Zaira and her sister Elizabeth, the happy-go-lucky friend from around the corner. Nancy lived behind me in the alley, and there was JoJo, the middle-school boy who gazed as lovingly and intensely at his phone as Narcissus at his watery reflection. To round out our crew was the unimposing Deanna, who surprised us all a few weeks later when she formed muffled sounds we swear were words. While they may not have been on anyone's first-round draft picks for a team to tackle the biggest challenges facing our neighborhood, that would soon change.

A few days into our entrepreneurial inquiry, the kids were asked what problems they would love to see disappear. They rounded out the usual suspects, like drugs, violence, racial discrimination, and fear of deportation, as well as a few humorous ones, like the feral alley cats that leave presents every morning in the kids' sandboxes. But there was one that stood out more than all of the others—boredom.

"The stupidest things I've done in my life I did when I was most bored," one of them said. No words have ever been more truly spoken by a teenager. Ever since the Sonic Drive-In next door to us was boarded up several years prior, these young people felt like they no longer had a place that they could go to and hang out with their friends face-to-face. The result of that boredom isn't as apocalyptic as our appetite for intrigue might desire. Sure, they admitted that after-school boredom leads youth to experiment in ways that lead to unintended consequences nine months later. And yes, boredom can lead to gangs and consumption patterns that cause juvenile obesity. But the young people said that for the average kid in Argentine, it just leads to a kind of mild depression. That's why they sleep after school and why they're endlessly stuck to their screens. They're shallow substitutes for the core cravings of adolescents—connecting face-to-face with friends and finding community and belonging there. The easy answer to their boredom might seem like getting involved in extracurriculars or getting a job. But it isn't so simple when they don't have any way to get there and back.

There was a second issue that our youth circled around: all of the empty storefronts in the neighborhood. The neighborhood has experienced the kind of disinvestment typical in many urban communities. Argentine once had a bustling business district with all of the charming characteristics of a small town. All that changed in 1971, when Indian Springs Mall was built a few miles down the road. The businesses along Strong Avenue shuttered. All of the life that was once here was sucked out like the pulpy dregs of an Orange Julius. Thirty years later, the mall too would close, leaving in its wake an urban wasteland devoid of commerce that wasn't liquor or payday loans. It bore not only an economic impact on our community but also a psychological one. "The empty storefronts make us feel like we live in a ghetto," they said. These youth were putting their fingers on the local symptoms of a systemic collapse.

We briefly toyed with the idea of dividing our group where half of them would attempt to address the problem of youth boredom and the other half would take on the problem of urban blight and empty storefronts. Yet very quickly, they realized that they cared about both issues. "What if," the youth wondered, "we create a youth hang out in an empty storefront?" The excitement grew. We went out on a walking tour of our neighborhood. There wasn't a dearth of options. There was a former car dealership with a for-sale sign on it; an old *tortilleria* whose owner had moved to Mexico; the vacant Carnegie library, which had given way for a newer one in the old Thriftway site; and a smattering of other spaces whose former lives were now accessible only in the memories of our most seasoned citizens. But there was one empty storefront that was the most appealing of all. It was a part of a strip mall shopping plaza that housed old cubicles and office furniture. It was adjacent to the new library, where many middle schoolers headed right after school already. If there was such a thing as prime real estate in our neighborhood, this was it.

Identifying a potential location was one thing. Yet they still hadn't described what the after-school hangout would be like. Rhiannon had the answer. Earlier that summer, she had attended our ministry's summer camp. Her favorite place to hang out was the snack shop. There, she escaped the heat with a swarm of other young people, eating ice cream, listening to music, and playing ping-pong and air hockey. After an impromptu field trip to the camp so the rest of the team could see for themselves, they saw what they were looking for. Their new venture, Snack Shack KC, was born: turn a vacant storefront into a cool place where youth could hang out with their friends with cheap snacks, within walking distance, and at a place parents could trust.

During the question-and-answer portion of their pitch night, the executive director of an influential local nonprofit and school board member said, "You know, we've got a lot of programs in Argentine that we do for youth. We're always doing it *for* them, but never *with* them. But I'm seeing something truly different in this." She was right. So many youth programs claim to be about empowering youth, but oftentimes it's just a veneer. More often than not, youth leaders still attempt to steer youth toward ends that fit the agendas of the adults in the room. Rarely do we hand over the reins with a promise that we'll support what they want to achieve. But what interested us more than the school board member's commentary was that the storefront that housed old cubicles next to the library was owned by the school district itself.

The kids grabbed her card. In the ensuing months, they did the rounds with other school board members, who likewise were enthusiastic about the prospect of filling their vacant building with kids rather than old office furniture. They said the key was to convince the chief operating officer of the school district. A year out from their pitch night, the kids were sitting in one of the most powerful government offices in the city, sharing their dreams with the COO. She was sympathetic to our kids' dreams but also skeptical, with all of the adult concerns that have maintained the status quo of an abandoned main street for decades. Who would be liable? Won't gathering kids together actually create more problems? How can they ensure safety and security? How could it fit into the district-wide improvement plan that was already in place?

Our kids were deflated but undeterred. People will only be accountable and committed to what they have a hand in creating.[1] Had it been my idea to create a youth hangout, they would have abandoned this from the start. The only reason it had gone this far was because it was *theirs*. The students added to their business plan, talked to school security officers, and solicited letters of support from the library administrators, who were only too happy to off-load rowdy middle schoolers to someone else. We sent the updated plan to the COO. We waited. We heard nothing. The kids no longer believed it would happen, but nearly every week, we'd send an email asking for updates on her end as well as sharing new additions to our plan. Like the parable of the persistent widow, we knocked and knocked and knocked. After weeks of no response, I emailed her again, requesting action that would either move this forward or quit stringing these kids along. I copied a school board member who is a pastor friend of mine. He responded by asking the COO when this was going to happen. She immediately replied to meet her at her office the following week to sign the lease agreement.

More than two years after our kids nervously pitched their dreams in a library conference room, the grand opening of Snack Shack KC was actually happening. They were high school students who started their own brick-and-mortar business, giving life to a lifeless main street. They made me feel as if winning Super Mario Bros. wasn't quite as spectacular of a high school accomplishment as I'd believed it to be. The night of the grand opening, we got the obligatory giant scissors to cut the ribbon, local TV crews came in, and the building was packed with kids. We've been sold a story that teenagers don't have an attention span that lasts any longer than a three-minute YouTube video. But that night, these kids proved that they'll stick with something for months, even years, to make their dreams into reality.

What's Youth Ministry Got to Do, Got to Do with It?

One thing I didn't expect after the grand opening of Snack Shack KC was the number of people who said to us, "Wow! What a great place for you to do youth ministry from!" A handful of churches and youth pastors reached out and now wanted to meet there. I bit my tongue. What was lurking in the back of my mind was "What do you think we've been doing for the past two years? Was that not 'youth ministry'?"

Implicit in their response, I knew their answer: no, it isn't. It's admirable, exciting work. But to them, there isn't anything obviously "spiritual" about helping young people dream about creating a different kind of future out of the ashes of their neighborhood. What does discipleship have to do with design thinking? Where is God among slide decks, business plans, and meetings with school board members? It's great stuff, they concede, but they tell me they're more about "the work of the church."

If we wanted to start a ministry to young people in an under-resourced neighborhood, we might follow a more traditional logic that would go something like this:

Step 1: Find a place to rent in our neighborhood that is centrally located where youth naturally gravitate to. It might cost us a premium, but as we know, the real estate dictum doesn't lie: it's all about location, location, location.

Step 2: Attract them to our youth room with cool games and free snacks and drinks. This is especially necessary in a neighborhood without a lot of money.

Step 3: Form a youth group that meets for amazing worship and powerful teaching. Kids have short attention spans, so keep it catchy!

Step 4: After we have built a strong core of leaders, think about what we can do to bless our neighborhood. Finally, we have kids who are mature enough to think outside of themselves, and we can go on mission together.

What is most telling is how this formula reveals what we believe is indispensable to ministry and what we believe is dispensable. The past decades of youth ministry have shaped our imaginations to believe that what is truly essential to "real" youth ministry are gatherings where there is teaching of God's word and worship. Small groups are great. Prayer is great. Mission trips have their place. But all of the icebreakers and chubby bunnies in the world are there for one sole reason—to bring kids together for teaching and worship. Everything else is secondary. It's scaffolding. When this happens, the gospel message gets reduced to a spiritual form of salvation sometime in the future when we die, and youth are left wondering if God has anything to say about the material world they inhabit and the brokenness they encounter while moving in it.

Youth pastors' sense of mission—the impulse to see and move outside of ourselves and do something about the brokenness we find there—is back-burnered. Mission becomes something that we do occasionally. We perform random acts of kindness by raking leaves for old people. We go on a mission trip to a place a few rungs lower on the socioeconomic ladder than we are. While we're there, we might execute some perfunctory home-maintenance projects that our middle-school students are wholly unqualified for. Or youth might share their faith in someone else's community as some kind of weapons test site. This kind of youth ministry communicates very specific messages about what God's mission is all about. The content of that gospel we pass on is either too anemic to make any dent in the biggest problems of our world or too atomic in its willingness to blow apart the delicate webs of the people and places it encounters.

If the four easy steps for developing a youth ministry outlined above bear resemblance to the dominant logic of contemporary youth ministry, then what I did with my local youth was backward. Our youth ministry didn't end with a question of mission; we began with it: What does it look like when heaven comes to our neighborhood? How does creation groan for liberation around us? The group began not with a strong, core group of leaders but with a group of kids who barely knew one another and knew little about the church. But the group trusted that somewhere deep inside of them (as in all of us), they knew that their world was not the way it's supposed to be and that it was crying out for someone to put aside the familiar excuses, put aside the apathy that dulls us into believing that our world will never be any different than it is, and do something about it—to proclaim good news to the poor that does not wait until death, to proclaim freedom for prisoners without deferring to a future date, to set free the oppressed who are living, right now, in some kind of darkness that *they*, the youth, have unique insight into that the adults do not. The youth group began with a question of mission rather than ended with it, and they followed where it led us. This is what young people should know about followers of Jesus: Christians are people who bring life out of places of death.

If we had followed a more conventional way of doing youth ministry in a neighborhood like the low-status one we live in, we might have rented a space where young people could hang out, found donors to help pay operating costs, and attracted youth to that place with entertainment, cool programs, and free snacks. But in determining what would be a blessing to the neighborhood, the youth created a concept that would attract their friends without gimmicks, be a sustainable business model that would create jobs for young people, combat urban blight, take away the loneliness of adolescence, and give younger kids an inspiring example of what they might also do following God's mission—all at the same time. Our youth ministry still ended up with the quintessential youth group room—only this one is subsidized by the school district. And when all was said and done, our organization still hired a youth pastor, who walks with youth in their pain and gathers them together for teaching and worship. It's not that telling our story doesn't matter to us; it does. Yet the content of the story that we invite young people to enact matters deeply.

Going Off Script with God's Mission

As a kid, my crowning LEGO-engineering achievement was an army helicopter. I remember carefully laying out the sorted and labeled cellophane packets on my bedroom floor. I meticulously studied the directions, double-checking my work after each piece was placed. The pride swelled up within me hours later when the last block was laid. I raised my helicopter up in the air, like Mufasa thrusting young Simba over the precipice on Pride Rock. But after a couple of days . . . that was it. While the helicopter was cool, it was limited in how I could actually play with it. It broke whenever I tried. So instead of disassembling it and reassembling the LEGOs into new creations like the makers intend, I just put the helicopter on a shelf, and it stayed there. It became solely an artifact that marked one moment of my childhood. My LEGO career was over.

My oldest son, Luke, started off playing with LEGOs a little differently. His career commenced with small LEGO kits—race cars, airplanes, loaders—and like me, he began by following the directions. But his younger brothers would inevitably destroy them, and after momentary howls, he'd wipe his tears and rebuild them again and again. At Christmas and birthdays, he'd get new sets—each bigger and more elaborate than the last. Luke's ability to follow increasingly more complex blueprints grew as well as his confidence in improvisation. Following directions and the well-laid plans of someone else soon bored him. So Luke would experiment and go off script, creating his own inventions.

Some of Luke's inventions were immediate successes, and some were failures—there were oversights in structural strength and mechanics that needed reworking. When a prototype was ready to go public, he'd show it off, explaining with impassioned gestures how his invention would remedy some banality in the industrial supply line. Emboldened by "wows" and accolades, Luke would turn around and march back to his workshop more determined than ever to design the most complex, overengineered solutions to solve the world's simplest problems.

Luke has a fluency with LEGOs that I never had. He has an effortless command of not only following complex directions but also breaking from those conventions and creating something new. Luke realizes that the true joy of LEGOs is not in playing with the static, fragile objects that result from his efforts but in the very acts of creation and invention themselves. Where I put my helicopter on the shelf to avoid it being broken, Luke accepts that breaking is part of the landscape. He can create and destroy without the kind of emotional investment or fear of loss I always had because he's done this again and again and again. It's a confidence born out of regular trial and error, success and failure, experimentation and risk, and knowing from experience that he'll create even something better than what came before.

The mistake ministry leaders made when they saw Snack Shack KC was that they marveled at the helicopter rather than the creative process. They wondered about the potential utility of the static object rather than the potential pent up inside of the creators. Now that we had gone through all of the hard (but secondary) work of building, we could actually do "real" youth ministry. But as Luke came to understand, the true joy and the true value of LEGOs are in neither the product nor the ultimate utility of the creation but rather the act of creating itself. In the ensuing years, Snack Shack KC has undoubtedly had a profound impact on the lives of hundreds of neighborhood youth. But perhaps some of the most valuable youth ministry is not in the product that has come for the masses but in how a handful of young people have been shaped for sacrificial lives of mission through the act of creating it. A more full-bodied definition of youth ministry is one that involves becoming fluent with God's mission through endless iterations of creation, destruction, improvisation, and failure.

For too long, youth leaders have approached youth ministry much like following LEGO directions. With relatively few sets in our repertoire, the instructions are the same—read your Bible, avoid sex and drugs, bring your friends to church or youth group, go on a mission trip, do a service project in the inner city. They're all just variations of the same prescribed formula. They require very little imagination; they simply ask you to follow the script. The consequence of all of this is probably something akin to my LEGO-building career—young people give it a try and never pick it up again. They get bored. There's little freedom to exercise their full, unique agency. Then those same young people become adults who feel halfheartedly about mission and think about it in the same narrow, unimaginative terms.

In its place, youth leaders can create the kind of environment for young people that allows them to go off script. Instead of following the traditional prescriptions for mission, we can unleash their imaginations for God's kingdom come to earth, encouraging them to build, create, and work toward not what someone else deems important but what matters to them. We can train young people to develop a fluency with God's mission because they have become accustomed to experimentation and failure. Through iterations of trial and error, they become confident enough to pick themselves up again, emboldened by the "wows" and accolades of caring adults all along the way. Perhaps it's these acts of creation—of breathing and bringing forth something out of nothing—that speak to those deepest suspicions of young people that they are indeed made in the image of God.

My friend Cole is a youth pastor in suburban Kansas City. He tweeted out a common conversation he has with students in his youth ministry:

> STUDENT: Everything is meaningless and boring.
> ME: What have you been working on creating?
> STUDENT: What?

It perfectly encapsulates the peculiar restlessness and dissatisfaction that young people face in our culture. The student doesn't even know what Cole means by the question "What have you been working on?" because it seems so irrelevant to the student's nihilistic confession. America's consumer culture has so shaped us through passive habits that we can't even imagine how generative habits of creation might break through the languor of his day-to-day life. The only remedy for boredom that we've been taught is entertainment and consumption—and when that no longer works, to do it bigger and better the next time. Yet we are most alive when we are caught up in the act of creating. Our senses are most fully engaged when we are cooking, writing, painting, building, repairing, knitting, inventing games, playing, and acting.

Youth ministry has been an enthusiastic handmaiden to a culture of consumption. Suburban churches have been sites of an entertainment arms race, offering bigger and better options as well as engaging in a fierce competition for an ever-growing market share with one another, sports, academics, and other youth programs. Not only has churchgoing evolved into a consumptive activity; its understanding of the gospel has become consumptive along with it. Once this gospel has been "received" into one's heart, it can functionally be set aside because it makes no further demands of us. The gospel is something that is passively believed rather than something that invites a participatory allegiance marked by habits and practices that move us toward the pain of the world and provide balm to that which cries out.

Heaven Is Coming to Earth

The baseline for a Christian identity doesn't have to be consumption. Youth leaders can lay new foundations where young people understand Christians to be those who join God as agents of restoration in the world. We might begin by resituating ourselves in the biblical narrative as a part of God's still unfolding story. If you ask the average young person in our churches about what the ultimate Christian hope is, after a panic-stricken moment where they feel like they should know the answer, they will commonly say some variation of "going to heaven someday." And yet when we go to one of our bookends—Revelation 21—there is a very different image of the future in store. Instead of people leaving a temporary home on earth to be with God in heaven, we see the reverse. We see God coming down to earth and taking heaven along. It's as if John of Patmos is witness to a long-forestalled marriage union between God and people, between heaven and earth, after having been violently torn apart, and a loud voice announces that this estrangement has come to a final end: "Look! God's dwelling place is now among the people, and he will dwell with them. They will be his people, and God himself will be with them and be their God" (Rev 21:3). Our final hope is not going to heaven. It's that heaven is coming to earth. We don't leave to live with God. God promises to make God's home here with us. And when this happens, God will wipe every tear from every eye, and there will be no more death, mourning, crying, or pain, for the old order of things will have passed away.

Youth leaders might ask themselves, What present order of things in the worlds of our youth needs to pass away? Together with young people, we can name the death-dealing forces that suppress the full flourishing and flowering of our communities. We identify the people and things that are trapped in mourning, crying, and pain around us. We keep vigil, seeking in prayer, listening to how God might be inviting the young people in our lives to join God among the wounded and crucified to share in their suffering and wait, long, and struggle for liberation with them. The culmination of God's story—that heaven is coming to earth—means that God has something to say to the pain we experience here. While people may dismiss it by saying "this too shall pass," minimize it by comparing it to the riches waiting for us in heaven, or defer it for a later date, God will not. God cares about the suffering of God's children *now*. God has created a new family *now* in order to exchange the label of "strangers" for that of "siblings" so that we might care for one another right now, even as we wait for the fullness of God's new order to finally replace the present one that crumbles in decay.

Revelation 21 and its language of an old order that will be replaced by a new order echo throughout Hebrew Scripture, holding deep roots in the Jewish imagination. The prophets described the present order as one defined by injustice, suffering, misery, and oppression. It was something that Israel had become quite accustomed to, in its history, when it was plundered by foreign armies and hauled off into exile. Yet even before external forces threatened Israel's existence, the Jewish elite rotted the core of the nation, destabilizing it from the inside. Those on the bottom end of the economic and social hierarchy felt the crushing weight of inequality.

Nevertheless, the prophets spoke of an end to the present darkness Israel faced. A new day would one day dawn where an end to premature death, fruitless toil, and violence would surely come. "Never again will there be in it an infant who lives but a few days, or an old man who does not live out his years," declares the prophet Isaiah. He continues, "The wolf and the lamb will feed together, and the lion will eat straw like the ox" (Isa 65:22, 25). The old order, characterized by the domination of the many by the hands of a few, was passing away, and a new order marked by justice, peace, flourishing, and communion would soon reign. The rabbis and ancient writers of the Talmud described what Yahweh was doing as *tikkun* (to repair or mend) *olam* (the world). The Jewish hope was that the coming Messiah would enter the brokenness of their world, gather the tattered garments and the shattered shards, mend them back together, and weave the world back to wholeness.[2]

The Christian hope is not altogether different from this ancient dream. Christians make the audacious claim that the Messiah had decisively come, entered into solidarity with suffering humanity, demonstrated boundary-breaking new possibilities for social and economic life, was executed at the hands of an unjust court in collusion with a corrupt state yet inexplicably rose from the dead three days later, forever upsetting the once-settled surety that death has the final word. Because of Christ's resurrection, the architecture of the old order has been fatally shaken. Its foundation is crumbling. A new order has been ushered in, and people have been called to participate in God's work of repairing the world as we gesture toward, wait for, and hope for that day when that bookend will be complete and God will make all things new.

A youth ministry whose hope is that God is reuniting heaven and earth sees one of its primary vocations as mending the world. Through specific habits and actions, we "practice resurrection" in the world. This cannot be secondary. Looking beyond ourselves and turning our faces toward a hurting world are not practices that can be postponed until there is a strong, committed core of youth who know God's word and are enthusiastic in worship. It cannot be something that we do sporadically whenever it fits into the cracks of our calendar or thought of as a special event that happens somewhere else but never in our own backyards. This is precisely the kind of religion that the Jewish prophets warned about.

Loosening the Chains of Injustice

The religious culture of the people living at the time Isaiah was written had all of the indicators of genuine interest in cultivating intimacy with God. People seemed eager to know God. They fasted. They had elaborate worship and great music. They held religious festivals. In short, they elevated the two primary activities—teaching and worship—that contemporary youth ministry defines as the true markers of "real" youth ministry and essential for Christian formation. But God wanted nothing to do with it. God wondered, How foolish and small of a god do you think I am that you think I would want this? "Is this the kind of fast I have chosen, only a day for a people to humble themselves?" asks the prophet Isaiah (Isa 58:5). Am I merely interested in gestures of piety, like bowing your heads and putting on sackcloth and ashes? No. God clarifies for the people in the back: "Is not this the kind of fasting I have chosen: to loose the chains of injustice and untie the cords of the yoke, to set the oppressed free and break every yoke? Is it not to share your food with the hungry and to provide the poor wanderer with shelter—when you see the naked, to clothe them, and not to turn away from your own flesh and blood?" (Isa 58:6–7). The teaching of Scripture, worship, and fasting—these are all good and essential elements of spiritual formation. But if they are not accompanied by justice, by loving one's neighbor as oneself, then they mean nothing.

The prophet Amos is even more incisive: "I hate, I despise your religious festivals; your assemblies are a stench to me. Even though you bring me burnt offerings and grain offerings, I will not accept them. Though you bring choice fellowship offerings, I will have no regard for them. Away with the noise of your songs! I will not listen to the music of your harps" (Amos 5:21–23). Israel didn't understand the assignment. The people thought they could get away with performing religious practices and habits that were ostensibly more spiritual while neglecting the seemingly earthly matters of justice and mercy. What did God want instead? It wasn't sacrifices or music. Amos's reply thunders like whitewater churning through a canyon: "But let justice roll on like a river, righteousness like a never-failing stream!" (Amos 5:24).

This is why we contend that many of the current forms of youth ministry need to die. If the world around us groans for liberation, longing for the children of God to be revealed, and if those children are to be agents of restoration, mending the world and bringing glimpses of God's new order through the cracks of the old, then the old order of youth ministry needs to pass away if it wants a part to play. The structures, habits, and practices of this old order built on an overspiritualized theology—all of this has to pass away. God has inaugurated something new in Jesus Christ, yet by treating justice as secondary and expendable, our practices and habits haven't changed from the small-minded popular religion of the time of the prophets.

In its place, youth ministry needs a new integration of our faith that combines a seamless matrix of our spiritual practices with actions to mend the world. It needs to be the practice of a faith where love for God and neighbor are inextricably bound up with each other. It will require the creation of a new culture and generosity for what counts as legitimate activity in youth ministry. We need to have the kind of openness to see tools such as asset maps, customer journey exercises, and venture canvases as ways to help young people discover how to encounter their world, nurture empathy for others, develop eyes-wide-open solutions that respect the dignity of the people they might help, and confront the enormity of these challenges without being naive. We can see these tools as ways to deepen our love for our neighbors that move beyond a childlike impulse to simply include others toward a more sophisticated inquiry into the complex systems that keep people down. This is in keeping with their adolescent capacities as well as their desires to be taken more seriously as adults. In the same way that we might expect more knowledge of Scripture, theological nuance, and church history from adolescents than we do from young children, our catechesis should expect more robust expressions of love for neighbor from young people as well.

Growing up in Love for Neighbor

There have been many critiques rightly directed at some humanitarian responses of prominent Christian NGOs—like providing shoeboxes for kids overseas—and the problematic language some of them use regarding child sponsorship and adoption. The critiques indicate that as a whole, churches are more equipped to put Band-Aids on the biggest problems facing the world than they are equipped to solve them. Part of this may stem from a gaping hole in spiritual formation, which trailed off somewhere in adolescence. Perhaps the truncated institutional responses to human tragedies are reflections of the individuals within them. Though well-intended, the responses remain childlike because the call to love our neighbor wasn't taken as seriously as the call to love God. People fall for the same trap that some practices are more ostensibly spiritual, while others are seemingly earthly (and therefore secular) and outside the scope of the church.

The same might be said about the peculiar unease and resistance in some quarters of the church regarding conversations of inequality or white supremacy. Christians don't recognize that at the very heart of our inquiry into the forms of inequality among us is an impulse to love our excluded neighbors more. To open our arms and make our circles wider so that every one of God's children can participate more fully in the abundance of God's creation. It is all the more baffling that this comes from Christians considering how the apostle Paul nearly reaches out of his letters to grab hold of and shake his readers, pleading with them that if Christ means anything to them, then they should do nothing out of selfish ambition or vain conceit. In humility, they should value others above themselves, looking at not their own interests but those of others. Paul wanted to be crystal clear through his insistence that if Christians are to be known for anything, it would be for their "other regard." He goes on to explain that whatever divine privileges Christ might have had, he knew that they were not to be used for his own advantage. Jesus set them aside and took on the nature of a servant—a slave (Phil 2:1–8).

In a world where upward mobility is a virtue, Christians must be vigilant in developing counterpractices to follow in the downward way of Christ. If we have the eyes to see it, we can see antiracism education as a form of discipleship—a road to a greater understanding of the unique headwinds of oppression that some must face and the tailwinds of privilege that enable others to move about with little effort. When we were children, we could sing of God's love for children of every color. But as we help young people mature in their faith, we can also help them mature in their understanding of systemic injustice. We can help them move beyond childlike definitions of racism as something that merely resides in the human heart to more complex ones that see that racism resides in institutions, boardrooms, landholdings, and bank accounts.

This is not to suggest that youth ministers in the church are to abandon their seminary training or traditional practices like Scripture reading, prayer, and solitude (ugh . . . and fasting!). Nor are we suggesting that we must now become experts in design thinking with degrees in social innovation or diversity, equity, and inclusion specialists. Not at all. We must unearth, from within our respective theologies and traditions, the kind of faith that is unmistakably good news for the world—especially so for the poor and marginalized. A kind of faith that is not consumptive but creative, inviting young people to join God in mending the world, replacing the apathy and violence of the present order of things that diminish life in our own communities. A kind of faith formation that grows more sophisticated in its love for neighbor as it does its love for God. And as this faith grows in love for neighbor, we borrow some tools, wisdom, and insights that have been used to construct and organize the world as it is so that we might organize a more just, beautiful world still waiting to be born.

Six

Confronting Adult-Sized Problems

Kurt Rietema

If Snack Shack KC provides a place of structure and intention for middle-school kids in my neighborhood to gather and reinvigorates a shared social life for young people straddling childhood and emerging adolescence during the school year, the summer break is its exact opposite. The social lives of young people in my neighborhood during summer months are whistling, tumbleweed dust bowls. There are a few isolated islands of friend groups who gather unsupervised in one another's homes. The majority of middle schoolers in my neighborhood, however, find digital oases where they connect sometimes with friends but many times with strangers to pass the lonely weeks of their summer vacations and feel some semblance of human connection.

Summer is a cruel in-between stage for these middle schoolers, where parents are out during the day in blue-collar jobs—working as landscapers, stucco contractors, house cleaners, and warehouse workers—so the household responsibilities of caring for younger siblings fall begrudgingly on their shoulders. In just a few short years, their horizons of opportunity open up like they have for their high-school-age siblings, who have exchanged their unpaid labors for remunerated ones, oftentimes joining their immigrant parents in their workplaces. But at this time in their lives, the summer days are spent blindly figuring out how to deliver caregiving responsibilities without guidance or apprenticeship on how to do so. Iliana—a seventh grader—vacuums, makes mac and cheese for her siblings, and saves her younger brother from all of the daily near-death encounters he creates for himself that every parent of young children is intimately familiar with. Her parents know this isn't the most ideal arrangement, but it's what they can afford.

For other middle-school kids, their summer breaks may not be consumed by traditional adult responsibilities like providing childcare for younger siblings—they just have to take care of themselves. While this may sound like an adolescent utopia, with endless days free from the constraints of adults telling them what to do with their waking hours, within a few short days after the last school bell rings, they are already craving some sort of structure and direction for their days. Two brothers, Tony and Manuel, live just a few blocks away from me. Unlike Iliana, they don't have younger siblings to take care of. Their parents are off working all day long, so they get up past noon after finally falling asleep around three in the morning. The rest of their days, they'll play video games and watch YouTube videos because their permission to leave the house hinges on the kind of trusted adult structure that is in place for them at school but not during summer. Kids are caught between the warring poles of their parents' anxiety, hearing both "Do something!" right alongside "But be safe!" There is little real imagination or investment from either party in finding a suitable answer that might reconcile these impulses. The resulting default mode is that video games become pseudo-babysitters—coping mechanisms meant to entertain and numb in the liminal spaces of adolescence.

Moving past the inner-ring suburbs a little bit farther to the south, the lives of middle schoolers during summer break are quite different. I have friends there with kids of the same age. One is on a baseball team whose winning record bumps it into a more competitive division. Others are doing art camps, 3D modeling, and spending afternoons with friends at their subdivision's pool and weekends at a lake house. Sociologist Robert Putnam has done extensive research on the changing patterns of childhood and approaches to parenting. While Putnam observes an increase in parental involvement in developmental activities (like reading) across class lines, kids from more affluent families receive about 1,400 more hours of developmental time from their parents than kids growing up in poorer families. What's more, the annual parental expenditures for cultural enrichment like books, music lessons, and summer camps are $5,700 more for affluent families than working-class ones. The lived experience of our neighborhood kids mirrors a phenomenon happening across the United States.[1]

This was the problem that neighborhood youth in one of our recent ImagineX cohorts wanted to solve. Their social lives were rich during school, but when vacation came, it would all evaporate in the scorching summer sun. At a time when presumably middle-school kids have all the freedom in the world to do what they want and be with who they want to be with, they found the opposite. They had nothing to do and no one to see. The parks were of notable concern for these young people. While our neighborhood has a nice patchwork of parks within reasonable walking distance, they're boring. The bathrooms are never open, there's little shade, the maintenance is minimal, the last upgrades landed somewhere in the late 1980s, and for the ones that have playground equipment, it's all geared toward little kids. In short, they're just not pleasant. Perhaps that's why on one of the nicest days of the summer, in the middle of school break, when every kid has had a chance to sleep in, our young people set out to do some qualitative and quantitative research. What they found were neighborhood parks that were functionally empty.

A year after the youth did their own research, the Wyandotte County government released a study of budget allocation to parks and recreation departments in comparable cities regionally and nationally. The suburbs neighboring the city spend from four to five times as much per capita on parks facilities and programming as ours does. Just as with Snack Shack KC, our youth had their fingers on a local manifestation of a systemic failure. Our county has the lowest spending on parks and recreation in the region, competing among municipalities across the nation for the dishonorable title of the worst public parks. It's no wonder why the lives of young people during summer break are so vastly different from one another across our metropolitan area.[2]

Yet instead of complaining about institutional collapse that is far more entrenched and beyond the abilities of young people to change, they decided to be creative. How could they make a summer to remember by amplifying fun in our otherwise boring parks? The youth identified three key elements that form a critical path necessary to create a successful venture: shade and snacks, equipment and activities, and friends to hang out with. If one of the elements were missing, it would all fall apart. They created a venture, Amp'd Up Summer, that organizes summer fun with activities and a mobile equipment library, keeps youth cool and comfortable with shade and snacks, and finally, guarantees there will always be new friends to have fun with.

At the beginning of the summer, the kids launched their project. An HVAC company donated an old van that they slapped their magnetic Amp'd Up Summer logo onto. They set up pop-up tents in the parks, rigged up with a misting system to keep cool. A local taco truck lent them a spare generator, which powered the sound system and the snow cone machine borrowed from a church. They set up a portable gaga ball pit made through an Eagle Scout project and had an arsenal of water guns and water balloons that they bought with a handful of donations. The first couple of weeks of summer break were glorious. They set out for the project to make it a summer to remember, and it was on course to do just that. Until it didn't.

Little by little, some of the elements that they'd defined as critical ran into snags. The parks and recreation department didn't open the bathrooms, so access to water was gone. The kids ended up playing the same games over and over without bringing in fresh activities, so they got bored. But the most fatal was the one that they knew was most important of all: the commitment to show up. The year before, we'd peeled back the onion to discover what was at the very core of disengaged youth in our neighborhood. Why would they weather loneliness—numbing it through video games alone in their homes— rather than take a risk on showing up to something they knew would be fun? They summed it up in a phrase: "I'll go if you go." We could remove every barrier: the risk of boredom, the cost, transportation, parental permission, and not knowing about it. All of those things could be addressed perfectly. But if a middle schooler doesn't have the assurance that one of their friends is going to be there too, there aren't enough gimmicks in the world to convince them to give up a familiar loneliness they have control over for the potential gain of social belonging. "I'll go if you go." That was the glue that held it all together. Then came the unexpected doctor's appointments, extended visits to family, babysitting responsibilities, or camp volunteering. Little by little, the social contract was violated until no one showed up and everyone sat at home. Miserable. Stuck to their screens. Just like the summer before.

Going Farther Than Anyone Else Before

There are plenty of drawbacks to living in an underresourced urban community (the funding of our parks and recreation department, for example). But by and large for my family, the blessings outweigh the burdens. One example of that was found in watching my own middle schooler, Luke, running in cross country and track meets this past year. Luke is a natural runner, with long, lean limbs (unlike his mother and I, which raises questions). He's been more successful in running than he has been elsewhere in more popular team sports. But I also love watching the kids for whom running doesn't come easily—the kids who are in track because a friend is doing it. The kids whose teacher and coach encouraged them to join more because they needed to field a whole team rather than because they saw some innate, diamond-in-the-rough qualities in them. What I love about living in this community is that there is a place for those kids to participate and push themselves in ways that they would never have been given a chance to in a more desirable school or more desirable zip code. As much as I love cheering for Luke, I love to cheer for those kids who are huffing and puffing for last place. They're chugging along in bodies that are probably more elegantly designed for some other tasks, but they're doing it. They show heart, knowing that the race was over from the moment the starter pulled the trigger but fighting as if they still have a chance. No, they won't win any awards, but the victory is that they showed up at all.

That's how I like to think about what the youth who attempted Amp'd Up Summer did. They might call it a failure. They did fall short of their own big dreams. But the miracle is that they attempted anything at all. Gordon Cosby was the pastor of the Church of the Savior in Washington, DC—an intentionally small congregation but one that had an outsized social impact on their city through affordable housing initiatives, jobs programs, and walking alongside addicts. Cosby put it this way: "The most helpful experiments are accomplished by people who are too naive to know what they're getting into. The wise and experienced know too much to ever accomplish the impossible."[3] No, these youth didn't eliminate the boredom and loneliness that middle schoolers in our neighborhood feel over summer break. They couldn't fix the budget allocation for the parks and recreation department, nor could our youth convince them to hand over a key to their precious park bathroom. But for a few short weeks, a couple dozen middle schoolers and their siblings felt joy. They felt belonging. They laughed. They played. For a few fleeting breaths, they lived in a fantasy where the momentary rules of their world were suspended, and they felt free. Then it was over. They didn't accomplish what they had set out to do to make it a summer they would remember, but they went farther in ending loneliness than anyone else before them ever had. The rest of us know far too much to have ever even tried in the first place.

You Are Only a Young Man . . .

For forty days, an absolute giant of a man stretched out his full nine-foot-nine-inch frame in the morning on a hill in Judah. From there, the Philistine hurled insults across the valley, mocking the cowardice of the so-called people of God. Goliath called out for a tribute from Israel to settle the conflict in *Hunger Games* fashion. Send your best warrior and drop the gloves—no one else gets hurt, but we'll probably enslave your wives and children after we defeat you (see 1 Sam 17).

King Saul and his merry men cowered in fear like neglected kennel dogs on the opposite hill. The giant's insults were a corrosive acid, dissolving the spirit of Israel's army and leaching doubt into the foundation of its once-solid trust in God's protection over it. Israel second-guessed its own history. The people told stories about how God made a way out of no way, with the Red Sea before them and the Egyptian army hounding them with hot breath behind them. They regaled with tales of Gideon defeating a Midianite army of 120,000 with nothing but trumpets and jars in the hands of Israel's 300 dumbest soldiers. But standing face-to-face with Goliath sucked out all of the bluster and romance from their campfire songs, making them wonder how much those stories were studded with myth and legend. And every day, the giant goaded them, needling them where it hurt most and perforating the last bits of pride that remained.

The Philistine reduced the people of the God of Abraham, Isaac, and Jacob to functional atheists. If no one in Israel was willing to blindly bet that God would prevail against the giant, King Saul would have to revert to another time-honored tactic: bribing them. The king promised riches, his very own daughter, and to lure in the true conservatives of the bunch, exemption from taxes. Still, no one took the bone. Then the teenage shepherd stepped onto the scene.

David's arrival hacked off his brothers, who thought the kid shirked his duties to his sheep because of some voyeuristic curiosity to see blood and gore. But the only thing David did see was a bunch of men playing dress-up and refusing to play the actual roles of soldiers. David had seen enough. Word got back to King Saul that there was some kid who was mouthing off as if he was going to step up and fight him if nobody else would. Saul was some kind of desperate, so he sent for the kid.

David walked over to King Saul. David was deferential enough to the king's office but resolute with an "I said what I said" attitude. Don't let anyone lose heart. I'll fight him. King Saul respected the kid's pluck, no doubt. If only one of his seasoned soldiers had half of the chutzpah that this kid had, they wouldn't be sitting on this stupid hillside every morning eating shame for breakfast. You can't fight him, Saul responded. You're only a young man, and he has been a warrior since his youth. Sounds familiar. How many times have our young people heard some version of that?

I love David's reply. He didn't have the creds of one of Saul's soldiers. But does the king know the kind of stuff that a shepherd has to face? David explained, "When a lion or bear came and carried off a sheep, I went after it, beat it, and rescued the sheep from its mouth [*its mouth!!!!*]. And when it turned on me, I seized it by its hair, struck and killed the savage beast. I've killed lions and bears, so yeah, I think I can take on an uncircumcised Philistine. The same God who rescued me from lions and bears will rescue me from him" (1 Sam 17:34–35; paraphrase).

King Saul saw that David wasn't joking. Nor was he the child he'd first believed him to be. Maybe there was something here. Saul gave David his blessing. He would do even more: Saul dressed him in the king's own armor. David looked ridiculous. He was as clumsy and weighed down by the battle armor as a peewee football team suited out in NFL gear. This wasn't going to cut it. David wasn't used to it. He would use his staff and a slingshot—protection familiar to him in the sheep pasture.

The rest of the story has been told over and over again. Goliath saw that Israel had sent a child out as their champion, as much annoyed as he was offended that this was the best they could send. David knew how to curse like a shepherd in response, threatening to cut off his head and feed the carcasses of the Philistines to the wild animals. As Goliath charged, David reached into his pouch, grabbed a smooth stone, slung it around, and struck the Philistine square in the forehead, who keeled over like a giant sequoia crashing at the lumberjack's feet. The witch was dead. The curse that hung over Israel had snapped. The shepherd boy defeated the warrior giant.

These are the stories that furnish the childhood imagination in churches. They grip us with wonder and fill us with the kind of faith that says that there is a God who stands up to bullies that taunt and terrorize the weak. Yet somewhere along the way, as church leaders help students make the turn into adolescence, youth pick up the idea that childhood stories are somehow *childish*. It's as if a rite of passage into adulthood requires disenchantment, and in the vacuum of mystery, they fill the void with coolheaded rationalism. But these stories contain so much insight into both the ways our communities dismiss the embryonic capacity of youth and how we might channel their nascent frustrations with the world, fueled by an innocent optimism not yet blunted by repeated, failed attempts to correct it. Make no mistake, the cynicism that has calcified our cultural imaginations requires the kind of naive energy that youth offer to break its curse. And perhaps we might recapture the original glory of those childhood Bible stories a second time not through reenactments in a Sunday school classroom but through real-life role-playing where young people attempt to conquer the Goliaths that threaten to engulf them.

For all of the talk that we have, as youth workers, of a steadfast belief in empowering young people in our care, what I think will be required of us to venture out into new pastures will test the limits of our trust. We have grown quite accustomed to youth being dismissed not with the outright mockery of a Philistine but by being subjected by many adults to the kind of "oh, honey" chronic underestimation demonstrated by King Saul. We are not exempt. We're going to need a different kind of posture than we're used to, one that hands over the reins of leadership to youth in a substantive rather than gestural way.

Are You Ready?!

I saw the difficulties of adults' willingness to make space for youth leadership firsthand recently as I led another ministry's middle schoolers through our ImagineX journey. Over the course of six weeks, we immersed ourselves in an imaginative reading of the book of Nehemiah. Nehemiah provides a perfect archetype of a change-maker and the journey of ups and downs that one might encounter. During each session, we then turned our gaze outward to the world around us, plumbing the depths of pockets of pain in our midst. The youth named many of the more obvious problems that young people care about, like homelessness and, yes, boredom. But in a brave act of vulnerability, they also named the mental health issues facing Latino kids like them. As they played around with potential answers to these crises, they knew. This was the issue they wanted to take on. Their energy swelled. Ideas emerged on how to address serious issues with fun—an emotional support animal petting zoo, a nerf war on (feelings of) terror, dodg(ball)ing our emotions, coping through crafting, a meditation station. There was no stopping them now.

Before we ever began, I had multiple conversations with the organization's staff and interns who would be with the youth every day in this process. We had no idea where the youth would lead us. But that was the beauty and mystery of it—the unfolding story of their passions crossing paths with the pain of the world. It's following Jesus to discover the hurt hidden around them, ducking down into the rabbit holes wherever they might go. Were they ready for this? On the shores of Lake Galilee, Jesus told Peter a hard truth. When he was younger, he went where he wanted. But following him at this point meant that someone else would lead him where he didn't want to go (see John 21:15–25). That's why I pressed the question with the adult leaders. They had been used to calling the shots. Did they know what they were being invited into? Were they really ready to be led by their youth to places they might not have chosen to go?

On the night of their pitch, the young people's parents gathered together to hear their kids' dreams out loud for the first time. And they didn't disappoint. They were winsome, funny, confident in their venture, and convincing about the need for what they had to offer. But when it came time for the questions and answers, I saw the first signs of a fracture. One of the ministry's board members asked about duplicating what other school clubs were already doing. Another staff member asked what professional therapists have already committed to helping. Knowing glances among the staff members who I'd worked with every day were exchanged. They were committed to going where the kids would lead, but it appeared that the senior leadership of the organization was not. Emails from board members went out overnight: What kind of liability would this mean? How does mental health fit into their values? What does Jesus have to do with any of this?

We might not be ready for the wily ways of God's spirit to break us out of the approaches to youth ministry that we have grown comfortable with and accustomed to and allow youth to lead us. Though it's tempting to heap trash on King Saul (he deserves his reputation), he turned quite quickly. Saul heard David out. Though he was young, Saul recognized that David was no slouch. Though David billowed over with bravado, he showed the receipts to back it up. He'd seen hand-to-paw combat in the fields with both a lion and a bear. Could a giant be exponentially more lethal than those? King Saul took the youth seriously when everyone else had written him off. When his brothers could only see his deficits, King Saul gave David his blessing. When the others could only see how David was lacking and not ready to take on anything serious, Saul recognized that the small victories in the sheep fields might open up a possibility for success on the battlefield.

We need to consider how we take young people in our care seriously, like King Saul did with David. When everyone else writes them off, we don't trample on their dreams like the rest. We must have eyes to see what others cannot. We see assets in our young people when others see deficits. The staff who worked most closely with these young middle schoolers saw something in them that the board members and senior leadership could not. My friend had known one of the middle-school students, Juan (name changed), since fourth grade. She distinctly remembers being over at their apartment while Juan and his siblings filled out a state trauma assessment. The kids' parents had been in and out of their lives erratically. On this occasion, they had been dropped off on his aunt and uncle's porch like a bundle of Amazon packages. Not long after, deportation would make the separation more permanent. With a trauma score of four or more on the Adverse Childhood Experiences (ACE) assessment, one's risk for physical and mental health problems as well as a tendency toward destructive habits like drug and alcohol abuse all increase. As my friend looked across the table, she saw factory-line consistency, with check marks affirming abuse, neglect, and dysfunction in nearly every way.

Juan had trouble in school. He was in and out of the principal's office. The teachers had him labeled, so before he ever had a chance to prove otherwise, Juan already lived in the category of "problem child." But my friend noticed something happen to him over those six weeks where they explored the biggest problems facing their community and were free to imagine what life might look like had those dark clouds lifted. She noticed that there was a new lightness, a playfulness in Juan that only came out when he felt safe. There was some power in connecting with kids with similar experiences. Because he was an expert in the subject matter, Juan realized his voice mattered, and he became an active participant. His energy was contagious. "That's the difference between being a problem kid and an influential leader," my friend reflected. She saw in Juan something the board members did not. She didn't see Juan's trauma as inevitably leading down a school-to-prison pipeline like so many others' had. She saw the domestic violence and neglect as the lions and bears he had beaten away in the fields, making him ready to face off with giants. There was so much more latent potential bound up in him if only he was given the opportunity. If only some of the stable adults in his life would fan the embers glowing inside of him. Our young people are looking for adult permission even when they don't realize it.

Not only did King Saul give David his blessing; he didn't leave him empty-handed either. Saul kitted him out with his very own armor. In the face of obviously determined young people, there can be a way of giving them our blessing that is actually just washing our hands of whatever comes their way as a result. It's not a promise to support them; it's a promise not to get in their way. But King Saul didn't do that. He was personally invested in David's endeavor. Saul knew that Israel's success was bound up with David's success. So he lent him the best of his armor, his knowledge of combat, and whatever it would take to empower the young man. But David wasn't feeling it. The armor was heavy and cumbersome. David knew his advantage over the giant was that he was more nimble and agile. He had to stay light and quick like he was in the sheep pastures.

In my work in helping young people make their dreams come alive, the most dejecting, dispiriting people are those that do them the honor of listening to their dreams but then immediately burden them with the heavy, bureaucratic armor of the adult world. You want to have a "wreck room" in our ministry center? The insurance underwriter is going to have to weigh in on this. You want to create a space for youth to hang out after school on school-district property? You'll have to provide a security guard and talk to community policing. Youth leaders need to listen to the dreams of our young people without immediately burdening them with all of the traditional barriers that we have to face in the adult world. Those shields have their proper place. They are often there for good reason—to protect us—but they can serve to protect the status quo if they are the first things young people are confronted with.

The Rules of Improv

In her memoir about the first half of her career as a comedian and sketch writer, Tina Fey lays out the basic rules of improv. The first rule is always to agree and say "yes." Whatever your stage partner has created, your job is not to question it but to say "yes" and play along. The second rule is to say "yes, and." It's a way of agreeing with what your partner has created but then adding to the story yourself and making your own contribution. The third rule is to make statements, not ask questions. The worst improv partners are those who point out all of the problems or contradictions of the stages that have been set by their partners. Fey's advice is that whatever the problem, be a part of the solution. The final (and what Fey calls the "best") rule is that there are no mistakes, only opportunities. She explains, "If I start a scene as what I think is very clearly a cop riding a bicycle, but you think I am a hamster in a hamster wheel, guess what? Now I am a hamster in a hamster wheel."[4]

These rules of improv lend themselves to our work as we listen to young people share their dreams with us. Whenever young people build up enough courage to bear their hearts, our first rule is to agree and say "yes." They say they want to open up a youth hangout in an empty storefront? Guess what the answer is? Yes! They want to address the mental health crisis among Latino kids that adults haven't cracked the code on? The answer is yes! They want to create an app to end boredom, and you know you could apply apps already in use toward it? Guess what the answer is? Yes! Your turn to add your own contribution to the idea will come soon enough, but your first response is "yes."

If the most dejecting and dispiriting people are the ones who burden young people with the bureaucracy and red tape of the adult world, then the most heartening people are the adults who hear their dreams and follow the "rules of improv." When the young people behind Snack Shack KC needed to get a permit to open up their storefront business, they ran into some snags with the building inspectors. There was a bathroom that was handicap accessible, but it had an electrical panel in it and therefore didn't pass the code. There was no mop sink. The entry doors opened in the wrong direction. This was an impasse that would normally cost thousands of dollars to rectify. The changes would be a death knell for my kids' dreams. I met with the head building inspector about the matter. From other projects I'd worked on, I knew he had no reputation for being pliable. But he recognized what was at stake. This wasn't a developer trying to squeeze by on the cheap. His word was the difference between the dreams of kids from a low-income neighborhood like he grew up in coming to life or not. He turned to one of the other building inspectors and said, "This isn't a bathroom, so it doesn't have to comply with the code. This is a 'toilet room.'" He picked up his notebook and left. The plans were approved.

Where everyone else saw a mistake, the building inspector followed the last rule of improv and made it an opportunity. Where we obviously saw a cop riding a bicycle, he saw a hamster in a hamster wheel. The head building inspector followed the kids' playbook, and he improvised to make it fit the rule book. Who were we to ask questions? Had the same ideas of our young people been brought forward by capable adults, they would have the book thrown at them. But we have met so many adults who are eager to open their doors and listen to the dreams of young people, leveraging their power to cut through red tape and make it happen. Young people have opened doors for our ministry that had been closed off to us. We've had so many times where we've felt like we've ridden on the coattails of our young people, not the other way around. Because of their efforts and leadership, our entire ministry has benefited.

A Time for Daring, a Time for Caution

There could be a certain kindness in Saul's response of wanting to protect young David from consequences his adolescent brain hadn't (or even couldn't) fully assess. King Saul knew what every soldier on that field knew: the price of failure wasn't embarrassment and a good lesson in humility. It was death. The stakes for our young will not be that high. Nevertheless, youth leaders do have a responsibility to warn young people who are acting foolhardy or taking on challenges that they are not (or at least not yet) ready to take on.

This is what John Keating, the inspirational English teacher played by Robin Williams in *Dead Poets Society*, warned his young pupils about when they misinterpreted his rousing lesson on carpe diem. After one of his students in their private all-boys school pulled a silly stunt during a school assembly pushing for girls to enroll in Welton Academy, Keating entered the room where the instigator, Charlie Dalton, sat self-assuredly in a leather chair with the other boys crowded around him like he was a celebrity. Yet instead of receiving an expected adulation from his favorite teacher, Dalton was handed a reprimand. He was confused. What was all of Keating's talk about seizing the day and sucking the marrow out of life about? Keating explained pointedly but lovingly, "Sucking the marrow out of life doesn't mean choking on the bone." He paused and continued, "There is a time for daring, there is a time for caution, and a wise man knows which is called for."[5]

Young people, just like Charlie Dalton and his friends, want adults in their lives who inspire them to seize the day. To make their lives extraordinary. To help them believe that another world is possible. That giants can be slayed with a single stone. And do this we should, for there are not enough of those voices in their lives. But we also need to know what the moment calls for. It isn't so much that we need to protect them from failure or even embarrassment. As highlighted earlier, there are great lessons to be learned from fighting for yet failing to reach their dreams. But we need to let them know when they are outmatched. When they're not yet ready. We need to let them know when they're about to make a spectacular mess for themselves and other people. We need to help them discern what the moment calls for, all the while being keenly aware not to project our personal hesitations onto them.

Dangling Carrots

Every day when Goliath stepped out onto the field and taunted the Israelites, the soldiers' impotence and cowardice were exposed. The stalemate on the battlefield reflected the deadlock within each soldier. There were warring parts of themselves both foaming at the mouth with indignation at the Philistine and simultaneously immobilized in a prison of fear and doubt. The king recognized this and dangled sparkling carrots before them: sex, money, power. But none of them worked. There were no external motivations powerful enough to end the standoff. They would be neither selfless warriors nor paid mercenaries. It was David who ended the forty-day cold war. Yet neither was his action animated by external rewards. Instead, David appears to be fed up with the disgrace. He was tired of the bullying, the disrespect, and his God's name being dragged through the mud. There was some primal longing for decency, which the Philistines had violated, that was motivation enough for him to act. Money would not do. The only reward worth fighting for was the recovery of Israel's stolen dignity.

Youth leaders have grown used to dangling sparkling carrots before young people because we've come to believe that they are the only things that will motivate young people to do the things we want them to do. And perhaps getting them to do what *we* want them to do highlights one of the root issues. We don't want to give up control. Like with King Saul, it's as much a lack of trust in God as it is a lack of trust in our young people. Every young person—some in big ways, some in small—has already been wounded by the unfairness of our world. Sometimes it happens just beyond their own consciousness of it—a back turned to them; a critical, penetrating, head-to-toe assessment in a school hallway; a barely concealed snicker from the adjacent cafeteria table. Each young person has experienced and witnessed a thousand nicks and cuts, little injustices that they know deep in their bones are not the way it's supposed to be. Inside of every young person is a dream for a world made right. Somewhere, they still hold on to a fairy tale belief that some benevolent wellspring of goodness will send an unsung hero of humble origins on a perilous journey to do battle against the forces of evil and break the present curse that overshadows them.

Youth leaders have the opportunity to come alongside them and exclaim, "Yes! Yes, you were right all along! The good news is that the fairy tale is not fantasy. It has come true. God has broken the curse!" We need to trust, like the author of Ecclesiastes contends, that God has "set eternity in the human heart" (3:11). This is the proper well of motivation that they should draw from. Young people don't need the external rewards that we dangle hypnotically before them. That's what the world at large attempts to do, selling us shortcuts that numb and entertain while the world is dark around us. Like with David, the only reward worth fighting for is the recovery of their lost humanity. They will be moved by their own desire for the elimination of some great injustice and little else. They just need adults willing to come along for the ride and say, "Let's do this."

A few months after the middle schoolers pitched their idea to address the mental health crisis of Latino kids, I received a phone call from one of the ministry staff members I'd worked with. Having believed that the young people's idea was dead on arrival after its ice-cold reception from senior leadership, I was taken by surprise when the staff member asked me if the kids in their ministry could borrow my lop-eared bunny and chicken that I brought earlier for a live-action teaser of the emotional support animal petting zoo. Later that week, they were creating space for kids to explore issues of mental health with four of the stations they devised earlier in ImagineX. I was happy to comply.

When the staff member returned the furry and feathered creatures later that night, he was ecstatic. Two of his adult mentors returned from their discussion groups in tears, saying it was the best thing they'd ever done with their kids. Never before were they so honest and vulnerable about things they were dealing with. One of the youth said they shared things with the group that they didn't even share with their own therapist. Perhaps the ministry leaders learned the "yes, and" rule of improv too late. But it was better than never learning it at all, or they might have missed out on this inbreaking event of God's spirit.

This is what I love about melding youth ministry with social enterprise. When we allow kids to dream God's dreams for the world, to consider the pain around them, and to heed the call and join God in the work of mending the world, they make the mission of God their own, becoming cocreators and agents of redemption. When we trust young people—getting behind their dreams rather than trying to get them to buy into our own—this is the kind of magic that happens.

Seven

Creating toward God's Future

Kurt Rietema

When Marty McFly stepped into his hometown of Hill Valley thirty years into the future, he was disoriented by a collision of the familiar and the new pummeling his senses on the town square. The café where he once faced off with Biff Tannen and his bullying cronies now appealed to customers with its "vintage" 1980s theme. The clock tower was still there, where Marty and Doc Brown harnessed 1.21 gigawatts of lightning to power the time-traveling DeLorean back to 1985. But now it was updated with a contemporary glass-curtain wall. More preposterous for Marty, however, were the flying cars zooming over the mall and the enormous great white shark threatening to swallow him whole until it disintegrated into holographic confetti at the last second. The screenwriters gave themselves license to be a bit outlandish with their imaginary town because it was so unthinkably far into the distant future, anything was possible. The imagined year was 2015.[1]

The neighborhood youth in our social entrepreneurship program watched that clip of Marty McFly entering a year when they were only eight years old. We named what new technologies had been birthed since 1989 that *Back to the Future II* got right and which ones still seemed ludicrous. Then I asked them to think about their own neighborhood. What would Argentine look like thirty years into the future? What would it look like if it veered from the present trajectory that it has been assigned? What if we rejected the script that had been handed to us—the one where our neighborhood is something from which we aspire to escape—and instead rewrote an alternate future where we'd rather live here than anywhere else in the world? What would that future look like?

The kids got to work, drawing out a cartoonish map of our main street. The library was there. The community center was there. But like the Hill Valley of 2015, our youth envisioned a mashup of the familiar and the new. Next to the grocery store was an amusement park. Clopper Field turned into a professional soccer stadium. Food trucks dotted Strong Avenue, and there were dog shelters for our strays. And there was a pool.

All understand the gravitational allure of a pool on a late-June afternoon. Yet there's an acuteness to that craving in our neighborhood. Though we live in a city of more than 150,000 people, there's only one public swimming pool. It's more than sixty years old. And the fifteen-minute drive from our neighborhood might just as well be fifteen hours away for a middle-school student who has no way to get there. The youth were entranced. If there was one change that they could make in our neighborhood, they had found it. They wanted a pool. I tried to talk them out of it. I want our kids to dream big dreams. I just don't want them to dream half-million-dollar dreams that can't ever come to fruition. I needed something to steer them away from it without me squashing it for them.

I often invite a longtime public official to share with the youth in the ImagineX program what it has meant for them to be change-makers in the city. On this occasion, the mayor of Kansas City,

Kansas, accepted the invitation. We gave him context for our program, allowing him to see firsthand what neighborhood youth were capable of with the example of turning an empty storefront into a thriving after-school hangout. The mayor painted an enticing picture of our neighborhood when he was a kid. He pointed across the street to a vacant lot where his dad's law office once stood. Next door to that, he'd go with his friends to buy baseball cards at a variety store. In the space where we were sitting were a barbershop (his first job), an ice cream shop, and a grocery store along the way. He would hop on his bike and see his friends, go to the park, or catch a movie. The mayor's story of our neighborhood sounded like stepping back into the Hill Valley of 1955, dripping with bubblegum nostalgia. The youth listening to the mayor's story wanted in.

The youth had a prepared list of questions for the mayor. Yet the dream most dear to them was the one that Javier nervously voiced: they wanted a pool. The mayor responded by telling them all of the pressures facing the community: the potholes in the streets, the sidewalks that need replacing, and the sewer lines that are more than a hundred years old in places. After reciting this litany of problems that clearly captured the attention of young people, as infrastructure always does, the mayor showed a real knack for working with kids by telling them that a pool was the lowest of his priorities. He did not know the rules of Tina Fey's improv.

After the mayor left, looks of defeat hung in the air. If I was looking for a way to steer them away from a pool, I certainly got one. But this wasn't it. I was dumbfounded by the mayor's tactlessness, and the kids were crushed. I told the youth that unfortunately, I get told "no" by city officials and people in charge all of the time. In fact, that's part of what we have come to expect. Sometimes, we use that "no" as a reality check. Sometimes, there's wisdom in the "no" that we hadn't considered before, and it's best to drop our first draft and go in a different direction. But sometimes, people in power say "no" because it's just easier to maintain the status quo than to do the hard work of making change. I asked the kids what they wanted to do with the mayor's "no." Diego spoke for the whole group. They were undeterred. They wanted a pool.

If I'm honest, I didn't see the problem they identified as much of a problem. Sure, having a public swimming pool nearby is a nice accouterment for oppressive Kansas summer days, but I had a hard time pinning a pool on Maslow's hierarchy of needs. Residents of Wyandotte County regularly conspire with bored local journalists to fill slow news days with the same complaint: Why is there only one 60-year-old public swimming pool for a city of more than 150,000 people? City officials have so regularly weathered this complaint that they've moved from a kind of commiserating regret to the sort of bloodless response our mayor gave to the youth. Maybe I'd been jaded too, slowly assimilating to the tired story that we can't have nice things. If amenities are what you're looking for, go to the suburbs. Like the mayor, I wasn't yet convinced that the lack of swimming pools was a "real" problem.

In what ways might a lack of access to a swimming pool have a genuine negative impact on the well-being of young people? It didn't take much research to find out they were onto something. Among eleven- and twelve-year-olds, Black kids drown at ten times the rate of white kids.[2] The biggest reason? Access to swimming lessons and swimming pools. It makes sense. If one has never been formally taught to swim and has had little opportunity to get comfortable and confident in the water, when they do get the opportunity to swim, the risk of drowning increases exponentially. That doesn't necessarily answer how access to swimming pools is broken down along racial lines. Through more research, the kids found that the reason has a curious history born right here in Kansas City. Before *Brown v. Board of Education* led to the desegregation of schools nationwide, the NAACP sued the city of Kansas City, Missouri, over the segregation of Swope Park swimming pool. The NAACP won. As pools desegregated across the United States, attendance by white swimmers dropped 90–95 percent. The result? Cities quit investing public money in swimming pools. Pools then moved to the suburbs, privatizing swimming through clubs, neighborhood association–owned pools, and backyard pools.[3]

The youth were curious if this had an effect on us, so we did a search for current homes for sale with access to a neighborhood or backyard pool. The results were astounding. The map revealed a flurry of red dots in the suburbs and a giant, yawning chasm over our city. Before our eyes, inscribed in space was evidence for what they intuitively felt—a veritable swimming pool desert. We'd been redlined from aquatic recreation.

What Do You Desire?

It's here where again, some might ask, "That's really interesting (and unfortunate) about the lack of swimming pools and its connection to racial injustice. But what does a pool have to do with youth ministry?" In short, it's about what young people desire. It's about what visions of the good life capture their hearts and their imaginations.

James K. A. Smith explains that the default way of thinking about Christian formation is one of acquiring information about God through Scripture. Christians think of discipleship largely as a cognitive, cerebral activity because of how we think about who we fundamentally are as human beings. For the past couple hundred years, we've been shaped by Descartes's idea that at our base, what makes us uniquely human is that we are "thinking" creatures—following his famous line "I think, therefore I am." If we understand human beings as thinking creatures, it implies that first and foremost, we are defined by thought and rational operations. It is our consideration of the world that determines right action and behavior. For Christian formation, this has meant that we emphasize the development of a proper "worldview." It has been the task of the church, then, to take up the intellectual work of developing a Christian perspective or lens by which we might understand the world and act accordingly.[4]

This is in contrast to Augustine's understanding of what it means to be human, which maintained that we are fundamentally *desiring* creatures. Smith, following Augustine, argues that "our wants and longings and desires are at the core of our identity, the wellspring from which our actions and behavior flow."[5] In an Augustinian conception of personhood, it is not "I think, therefore I am" but rather "I am what I love." Smith continues, "To be human is to be animated and oriented by some vision of the good life, some picture of what we think counts as 'flourishing.' And we want that. We crave it. We desire it. This is why the most fundamental mode of orientation to the world is love."[6] If we step back to consider how this translates to a young person's life, even our cultural tropes of adolescence point to a larger truth that they act more out of hot-blooded impulses rather than coolheaded rationality. Marketing agencies understand this better than we do, assaulting young people with images and messages of a good life that hinges on an acquisitive desire for their products.

The implication for Christian formation, then, isn't so much about knowing and believing as it is about desiring and craving, shaping our passions and loves in conformity with God's desires. Smith explains, "Jesus's command to follow him is a command to align our loves and longings with his—to want what God wants, to desire what God desires, to hunger and thirst after God and crave a world where he is all in all—a vision encapsulated by the shorthand 'the Kingdom of God.'" If human beings are desiring creatures, then we act and behave in conformity with what we love—our visions of a good life.[7]

The problem is that we can't understand what a *good life* means outside of the life and death of Jesus. It is a term that awaits content.[8] Through Jesus's many parables and teachings about the kingdom of God, he paints a picture of what a good and beautiful life looks like. The kingdom of God is like a great banquet where the respectable and important people of status declined the invitation, so the host turned upside down the familiar rules that excluded others, opening wide the doors to the poor, the blind, and the disabled. It's like a king who canceled the debts of those that owed him. In vivid metaphors and boundary-shattering encounters with marginalized people, Jesus described and embodied what a flourishing life looks like, where no one is left out or left without. He furnishes our imaginations with snapshots of an alternative universe where status seeking is replaced with solidarity and the pursuit of the individual good gives way to the common good. Jesus tapped into the ache and longing of a people tired, worn out, and left out, giving them a taste of another world where love, beauty, and justice reign.

When Desire Is Misdirected

The people who fought against the desegregation of public swimming pools were likewise driven by a particular vision of a good life. But their vision of a good life was the absence of people they considered undesirable. Their vision of a good life was one in which they would happily take the tax dollars of Black and brown households and then turn around and exclude them from participating in the public goods that their money created. And when the courts said white people could no longer legally exclude people of color, they retreated to their private confines where they could continue de

facto segregation. Their actions and behaviors flowed out of a particular vision of a good life where they were surrounded only by people
who looked and thought like them—a vision that is in stark opposition to the one that Jesus describes. Nevertheless, many (most?)
of the people driving segregation were white Christians. Christians
who went to church. Christians who read their Bibles. Christians who
went to Sunday school and learned "Christian" worldviews. They
acted not out of the information that they acquired in church but by
an exclusive love for people like themselves.

This is how Augustine proves that his conception of the human
person is more apt than a Cartesian one. Actions and behaviors are
not driven by knowing and believing but by hungering and thirsting
for the vision of the world that we love. And for Christians, the world
that we long for, the locus of our deepest desire, the treasure hidden
in the field that we would sell everything for, is what Jesus called
the kingdom of God. Smith asks, "Could it be the case that learning
a Christian perspective doesn't actually touch my desire, and that
while I might be able to think about the world from a Christian perspective, at the end of the day, I love not the Kingdom of God but
rather the kingdom of the market?"[9] At the end of his Sermon on
the Mount, where Jesus redefines what it means to be blessed and
living one's life in tune with the ethic and spirit of God's kingdom,
Jesus addresses those who profess to follow him but whose actions
say otherwise: "Lord, Lord, did we not prophesy in your name and
in your name drive out demons and in your name perform many
miracles?" (Matt 7:22). They were—like those described earlier in
the time of the prophet Isaiah—the kind of people with all of the
trappings of religiosity. They used the right words, and they practiced
supernatural wonders not found in most of our religious repertoires.
But Jesus saw through it. He responded, "Then I will tell them plainly,
'I never knew you. Away from me, you evildoers!'" (Matt 7:23). They

didn't love what Jesus loved. They practiced the right things, but their fruits—their actions and behaviors—betrayed them. Their love was misdirected.

When we unearthed the ugly history that explained why our city had only one sixty-year-old swimming pool, I realized why it all mattered. The young people didn't want access to a swimming pool because they are a bunch of whiny, entitled kids. They wanted a public swimming pool because they were driven by the desire for a world like Jesus talked about where no one was left out. They didn't want to eat the crumbs of another's feast off the floor anymore. They wanted chairs at God's abundant table for themselves. They had uncovered a very local, very specific manifestation of God's kids being shut out from enjoying the full goodness and joy of God's earth, and they wanted to do something about it.

Most of the local youth come from households with very sporadic churchgoing. Most of them wouldn't be able to recite Psalm 23. They'd spectacularly fail a quiz on the twelve sons of Jacob, and they'd never let you hear the end of it if you played some glib, contemporary Christian music number. But deep in their bones, they are longing—like the Hebrews 11 all-stars of faith—for a better country, a heavenly one. They are learning to love a world so shot through with the grace of God that weapons of war are turned into gardening tools and people from every tribe and every nation are invited to the wedding feast of God.

This isn't to say that a desire for young people to acquire biblical knowledge is misguided. On the contrary, it's just that instead of viewing the Christian story as a collection of moral aphorisms that help people get along (or ahead) in the dominant economic and social imaginaries, young people might enter our Scriptures as if they are a portal to another world—a place where they might be infinitely fascinated, their imaginations set afire, enraptured by a way of being human and living gently with the rest of creation. There, they might find themselves in a place they have never been but that feels like a home they long to return to. Perhaps, like Peter, they might catch a glimpse of a shimmering, transfigured Jesus—a world shining like the sun in a way they have never seen before—and their first impulse would be to say, "It's good for us to be here. Let's put up a shelter" (see Matt 17). Let's make this place a home. But instead of setting up camp in that transcendent, divine world, youth leaders would take young people by the hand down the mountain and back into the ordinary world, asking how God might be inviting us to illumine the immanent with the same glory we just witnessed. Caught up by a vision of heaven, we pray for God's kingdom to displace the hells here on earth. Moved by an encounter with love, we move to make love manifest. This longing for another world, then, isn't a desire to escape or abandon ship but rather is moved out of a deep love for the world we've been given. That world we truly love, however, is one that has been crucified with Christ. Its power structures that once knew only death have died and been reborn.

When the Good Life . . . Isn't Good

One danger of sharing stories of ventures created by youth from underresourced communities like mine is the temptation to think that this isn't applicable to youth ministry in more affluent contexts. Perhaps it is easier to identify brokenness in areas with urban blight, aging infrastructure, and the churn of vices that follow in the wake of concentrated poverty. Yet young people everywhere are looking for that third way, where divine transcendence and the immanent frame intersect. Though it may be held more urgently, this isn't something unique to my youth group just because of their particular economic and social location. All young people want to see the lavish, reckless love of the triune God come crashing into the brokenness of their world, resurrecting life from the dead by putting flesh on dry bones and creating streams in the desert. Or—in a revised translation of Isaiah—creating swimming pools in the desert (see Isa 35:6). It's just that youth leaders fail to recognize how the dominant economic and social arrangements hurt both those who ostensibly benefit from them as well as those who are more obviously on the underside. The formerly enslaved person turned abolitionist and preacher Frederick Douglass put it this way: "No man can put a chain about the ankle of his fellow man without at last finding the other end fastened about his own neck."[10] Yet when one enjoys the material and social comforts of being on the contemporary plantation owner's side of the global economy, it's difficult to see how corrosive it is to one's own soul and one's own well-being.

I witnessed this firsthand when I assisted in another church-based youth ministry innovation program. As part of a panel of outside experts, we listened to young people talk about the biggest problems and challenges facing kids in their church youth group and then give short pitches with the initial interventions they had conceived to address their problems. A young woman from one church in the South said, "There is a huge pressure to succeed." They suggested that an adult-to-youth or a peer-to-peer mentoring program could help young people cope in such an atmosphere. In the second pitch, another confessed, "There's so much competitiveness, teens feel that if they fail, they are failures." Their team put forth two ideas: a mentoring partnership as well as a makerspace that would be safe to fail and try again in. Those who gave the third pitch voiced the anxiety among their youth, saying they had a "fear of not being good enough to meet the expectations" of the adults in their lives and perhaps an open mic and storytelling night would be a good way to unpack their anxieties. The fourth team didn't waver in their similar identification of the problem, with one young man saying, "Youth today are feeling lonely, isolated, and stressed."

A pattern took shape. Youth who were isolated from one another geographically independently expressed nearly uniform concerns. With one exception, they held something deep in common: the churches participating in the consultation were largely white, affluent congregations in suburban contexts. Only the fifth church, one from inner-city Houston, deviated from the rest in identifying the problems their youth felt. Their youth felt divided because they go to different schools and don't have common experiences. They proposed a gardening and cooking club to celebrate their cultural heritages or tricking out a bus with fun activities that could travel from neighborhood to neighborhood to connect them. The affluent youth suffered from too many activities, too many enrichment opportunities, too many pressures and expectations. The youth from the underresourced neighborhoods suffered from too little. Maybe having too much is as bad as having too little. If this is the good life, it sure doesn't feel like it.

There's an old saying that if you see a fish go belly-up in a lake, you try to find out what was wrong with the fish. If you see a thousand fish go belly-up in a lake, you better take a look at the lake. The adage has always been helpful for understanding why poverty, crime, and undesirable social outcomes are so persistent in urban neighborhoods like mine. And it helps shift the focus away from some inherent character defect in individuals and cultures and instead externalize the problems to the rightful perpetrators. The reason that there are such consistent patterns is because of a systemic failure that almost guarantees any individual caught in its web will fail along with the masses. But what became clear to me that day, listening to young person after young person describe their own localized tales of pressures to succeed and fears of failure, was that they too were victims of a systemic failure. They were swimming in poisoned waters.

Privilege was killing both poor and rich, just in divergent ways. Thousands of affluent youth were psychologically going belly-up in the lake, victims of their own supposed success.

Whether there was an inability to name their entire economic and social edifice as dangerous or if they just refused to because of what it might imply, only those of us outside listening in to the kids on our panel could see and name it. While the youth cried out for something to save them from this body of death, abandoning it entirely was unthinkable—the material comforts were too amusing and too secure. The result was that all the innovations that they imagined were mere tweaks, minor adjustments that moved the dial to help them become better attuned to the frequencies of their world. Yet it is no measure of health to be well adjusted to a profoundly sick society.[11] Neither the young people nor their adult mentors could conceive of any solutions other than coping mechanisms.

The role of youth leaders is to shepherd young people to the good life—God's good life as defined and given content by Jesus. We are to point them to green pastures, lead them beside quiet waters, and guide them to right paths. To get them there, we first need to name when they're walking through valleys of death. To have our souls refreshed in God's good life means turning from dominant definitions of the good life marked by achievement and acquisition. What the youth from the affluent churches needed was help in saying "no." Saying "no" doesn't contradict the rules of improv. "Yes, and" means we can only add our twist after affirming what precedes it. The youth already expressed that they wanted mentorship. Perhaps what's truly innovative, in a culture demanding more and more and more, are mentors who help young people say "no." It frees us to think about innovation in subtractive as well as additive terms.

What I can't shake is the thought that these youth are the grandkids and great-grandkids of the same people who fled neighborhoods like ours in the 1950s and '60s to build their own American idylls in new communities with new schools and new swimming pools free from people who didn't look like them. They're the ones who inherited the segregated dreams, the realized visions of the good life from those that had gone before them. And yet when listening to these kids talk about how those same adults burden them with crushing expectations and anxiety, their good life isn't so good after all. Perhaps these material and consumer paradises are also wastelands for people's spirits and souls. While living inside the dominant social imaginary, it seems plain that the pursuit of this good life is obviously a superior one. Everyone around it talks about it, and outsiders want in on it. They have the best schools, the best homes, the best restaurants, the best workplaces. It acts as an echo chamber that reinforces the idea that this is as good as it gets. There is certainly allure.

Finding the Good Life Where We Least Expect It

Last fall, I had a minor parental crisis when I was personally confronted with the radically different experience that my son Leo was having out on the soccer field from those of other youth from more wealthy neighborhoods in our county. Sporting KC, Kansas City's professional major league soccer team, sponsored the construction of a sixteen-field mega sports complex not far from their stadium. We parked our car and walked our way past pristine, artificial turf fields filled with kids uniformly kitted out with their club gear practicing drills by experienced coaches who clearly knew what they were doing. Leo's team, however, was not playing on any of these fields. His team was playing on the sloping grass fields on the other side of the parking lot. There, he and his teammates would swarm around the soccer ball, moving about the field with all of the mysterious patterns and obscure intent of a Ouija board. Unfamiliar, anxious questions stirred in me. Was I screwing up my kid? Is he getting left behind? Shouldn't I be giving my kid the best opportunity to succeed? Because while those other kids are learning skills, discipline, and excellence early, our kids suck.

Those questions still hung in the air the next week when I brought him to his regular practice at the unfortunately named Kensington Park. As I sat on the crumbling, postwar-concrete bleachers peering through the rusted chain-link fence, I heard laughter across the dandelions. I saw their Nepali coach teasing them with the ball in a game of keep-away. I heard a half dozen languages and dialects—Salvadoran Spanish and Burmese Karen and soccer moms in hijabs speaking Somali. I saw working-class people enjoying watching their kids play a game with working-class roots on a field with no airs of pretense. I saw kids being kids. They played for no other end than because playing and moving their bodies are fun and humanizing. Perhaps Leo wasn't learning attack drills or defensive clearances like the kids on the MLS-level fields, but I saw another kind of formation going on. There was an implicit curriculum about what a meaningful life that isn't based on accomplishment looks like. In a society obsessed with excellence and excess, Leo was learning what "enough" means on a field that is unattractive but adequate. In a society where people feverishly position themselves in relationships congruent with upward mobility, kids from a dozen ethnicities were swimming in the gifts and laughter of others different from them. The immanent curtain was momentarily pulled back as I caught a glimpse of the transcendent. "The glory of God," insists Irenaeus, "is a human being fully alive."[12] These ragtag kids out on that tousled field became a living embodiment of it.

Though I envy other kids' good coaching and would cry if I ever got my hands on a proper schedule of games and practices, I wouldn't trade this for anything. I've tasted an economic and social order that

Jesus describes as the kingdom of God, and I have been ruined for anything else. I think this is what Smith means by saying that we can't just think our way to new hunger. We will never list out the pros and cons of living according to the values of the kingdom of God versus those of the market and rationally conclude that Jesus's way is better. It has to be experienced. It has to be touched. It's only then that we might see that we have settled for something less and that our ultimate loves have been calibrated in the wrong direction. Our visions of the good life have been deformed, and "unlearning those habits would require counterformative practices, different rhythms and routines that would retrain [our] hunger."[13]

Retraining my hunger and recalibrating my definition of God's good life came about through hundreds of these metanoia moments—turning from the seduction of a good life defined by acquisition, status, and leisure toward people and places effectively locked out from those promises. There's nothing novel in my journey. There's no secret sauce here. The way of Jesus has always been a movement toward suffering. Near the conclusion of his letter, the author of Hebrews gives readers across the Christ-following diaspora these words: "And so Jesus also suffered outside the city gate to make the people holy through his own blood. Let us, then, go to him outside the camp, bearing the disgrace he bore. For here we do not have an enduring city, but we are looking for the city that is to come" (Heb 13:12–14). In a cultural context where our image of the good life has been deformed and desensitized by all of the material amusements and pleasures we can imagine, we need to have it be recalibrated by the crucified Christ, who is present among the marginalized. Christ isn't in the temple; he is in the streets. Likewise, we must quit believing Jesus will always be found in our places of worship. We must quit trying to innovate the church. Like the animals who were brought to the temple as blood sacrifices but whose bodies were burned outside of the city gates, Jesus likewise identified with the physical as well as the social location of the disgraced and the damned. He suffered in a place outside of the gaze of respectable people, hidden behind walls to protect the consciences of those who had condemned him lest they be stricken with guilt, eaten from the inside out by suspicions of their own complicity. Jesus was nearly always found among low-status people—people familiar with sorrow—inviting them to imagine and enact with him a new kind of life, one with a new kind of social and economic order that is truly good.

Yet not only did Jesus once suffer outside the city gates; the author of Hebrews urges us to go to him outside the camp *right now*. The audacious implication is that Jesus is still present there. The passage has theological echoes of Matthew 25. Jesus tells a story where those told to depart from the Son of Man's presence were confused and rebuffed. When had they seen the king in need and ignored him? Jesus, unmistakably identifying himself with the hungry, thirsty, foreign, and imprisoned, replied, "Whatever you failed to do for one of my brothers or sisters, no matter how unimportant they seemed, you failed to do for me" (Matt 25:45). What these passages beg us to see is that we cannot know Jesus without knowing suffering. We cannot divorce love of God from love of neighbor. If we want to find Christ and the good life that God promises, we must look among our neighbors who suffer outside the city walls. It's only there—hungering and thirsting for God's justice, waiting alongside our marginalized siblings in eager expectation of God's liberation—where we learn to dream God's dreams for the world rightly.

To instruct us to go to Christ outside the camp means he's not inside the walls where we might first go looking for him. So much of youth ministry is obsessed with looking for God in ecstatic worship experiences, quiet times of personal devotion, Scripture reading, and prayer. All have their rightful place among historic Christian spiritual practices. But if youth leaders want to introduce young people to the living Christ, we must see it as equally indispensable to take young people outside of our camps, to become familiar with suffering, and to know the crucified people by name. Perhaps there we might recognize in them the face of the crucified Christ.

Much of what is being undertaken in Christian social innovation is ecclesial reinvention. Suggested changes amount to renegotiations of the church's posture toward their surrounding communities, their practices of gathering, and their liturgical habits. Underlying this is the anxiety of a church in decline. Innovation, then, is born out of an attempt to bend statistics of church attendance in more favorable directions. Yet I wonder if here too we are to pay attention to the call of the author of Hebrews to go to Christ outside the camp. The kind of innovation we're advocating for is innovation outside the walls of the church. Instead of investing more time and money in the ways we do church, we invite church leaders to invest time and money in broken places, in broken systems, and among broken people. Instead of renovating our youth ministries, let's renovate our communities and neighborhoods, identifying them as our arenas for making change. And that's exactly where our young people were leading us.

A Way Out of No Way

After the mayor waved off the kids' concern about our city's one tired public swimming pool—an ancient relic old enough to remember where it was when JFK was assassinated—they still wouldn't let it go. We'd unearthed an ugly history, tracing our pool-less present to racist policies and practices of the past that had effectively redlined our neighborhood from a public amenity found nearly everywhere else in the metro. Yet that knowledge didn't make it actionable. A phone call with the parks and recreation director revealed just how out of reach it was. He knew the problem. He told us that at one time, there were about six public swimming facilities across our city. But there wasn't the tax base to justify building new ones. A new public swimming pool would cost a minimum of five hundred thousand dollars, and the operating loss to the city on our current one tallied up to three hundred thousand dollars a year. He would love to do something, but his hands were tied.

Every time I lead a group of young people through this process of uncovering the pain in their communities, determined not to pass by on the other side, we arrive at a dead end. Sooner or later the path that was once so clear to them disappears into the bushes. The joy at the beginning of the journey grows weary. I used to panic when it was clear the kids were stuck. It was like being caught in a roundabout with no exit. But now I welcome those moments. Because when it feels like there is no way out, God shows up to make a way out of no way.

"Waiting is an attentive anticipation of, even preparing for, the event of God's arrival in the world," writes theologian Andrew Root.[14] Waiting is an acknowledgment that we cannot do this by our strength alone. Waiting means that we have taken steps in faith to move in closer proximity to the pain of the world, and there, standing in solidarity with those who suffer, we have reached the limits of human action. We have encountered powers so intransigent and obstacles so beyond our abilities to overcome that we wait not in despair but in hope.

This spirit of attentive waiting runs counter to what we often see in innovation and entrepreneurship circles, which commonly valorize human effort and ingenuity. With the rise of innovation and entrepreneurship in our broader culture, church leaders watch as thought leaders get TED Talks and *Wired* magazine features. Venture capitalists are elevated as some kind of modern messiahs that will solve every intractable problem, from climate change to the ever-elusive edit button on Twitter. The church in North America has largely parroted this cult of entrepreneurial celebrity, throwing themselves and their dollars at anyone who might save them from institutional demise and declining cultural influence. The danger, though, is that when those of us in the church have an inflated sense of our own capabilities and creativity, we begin to believe, deep down, that there's no one who's going to come and save us. We think we're speaking of God, but in truth, we're only speaking of humanity in a loud voice. Like King Saul's soldiers facing the fall of the house of Israel, those in the church become functional atheists. While we might ceremoniously gesture to the action of God, we don't really believe it. God is easily squeezed out of the equation.

Waiting, then, is a necessary practice to remind us that our strength is not our own. Like the believers gathered together in the Upper Room, confused and scared at their Messiah's departure while under real threats of extermination, we are instructed to wait. We actively wait for the coming of the Spirit, trusting that the present darkness will break and that God will do something new. We should not confuse waiting with inaction, nor should we see it as a signal of resignation. Karl Barth provides helpful clarity: "To act—to 'wait'— means just the opposite of sitting comfortably and going along with the way things are, with the old order of things." [15] We wait not out of apathy but out of an appetite for a new order of things that we could never accomplish on our own strength.

What waiting has looked like for me, in leading young people on a journey to mend their world, is being attentive to the moments when we are stuck and spinning in the mud. And instead of trying harder and pushing through, returning to the scripts and formulas that have worked in the past, we wait. In our lostness, we abandon not the problems that they care about but the tools whose usefulness has expired. It's a nod toward Jesus's instructions to his disciples, who he sent to proclaim the kingdom of God and heal the sick: "Take nothing for the journey—no staff, no bag, no bread, no money, no extra shirt" (Luke 9:3). They were to depend on their sustenance from energies outside of themselves. It would leave them open to surprise as they found breadcrumb reminders that this was not their work but God's.

As I waited with our young people—their vision of a swimming pool oasis in a desert evaporating into a mirage—an activity I'd never thought of before unexpectedly came to me. On the fly, I rolled out a sheet of white paper and drew a Dr. Seuss–like contraption, the Change-A-Tron 2000. On one end of the conveyor belt, the kids would feed their big, impossible ideas: the amusement park, soccer stadium, food trucks, and public swimming pools. The Change-A-Tron 2000 would then kick, whistle, and sputter—dissecting their ideas, morphing them, minimizing them—until it spit out a product on the other end that was a realistic and attainable, albeit miniaturized, version of what they put into it. The amusement park transformed into a lawn mower pulling a train of oil-drum cars, the soccer stadium turned into a sweet futsal court, food trucks became snow cone stands, and the public swimming pool sported wheels, making it portable.

Some creative energy broke out in the room that wasn't there before. The change was palpable. Something from completely outside of them hovered over the chaotic waters of their primordial ideas like the spirit of God in Genesis, giving them shape and breathing life into them. The kids were ecstatic. They'd seen something like this before—in their investigation of the segregated history of swimming pools, they'd come across photos of "swimmobiles." They were mobile swimming pools that were carted around the boroughs of New York City in the 1960s and '70s, turning truck trailers into places that gave underserved residents access to water in hot summers.[16] They imagined what it would be like if they did something like that in their own city.

It turns out that portable swimming pools weren't just a stop-gap measure for parks and recreation departments scrambling for solutions in a segregated past. The city of San Diego has been operating a portable pool program since 1968. By the next week, the young people were on the phone with the director of the program, learning how they operate three sixteen-by-twenty-six-foot modular pools running for three weeks at a time in eight underserved neighborhoods. Fifteen kids splash around in thirty-minute sessions, taking swimming lessons every day for a week. Back-to-back sessions mean more kids without access to a traditional public swimming pool gain confidence in the water and know the joy of playing around in it on a hot summer day. What's more is that portable pools allow them to serve thousands of kids at an operating cost that is half the price tag of the annual loss of our public swimming pool. The youth had found a model that not only was affordable but whose viability has a proven track record going back more than fifty years.

The youth group set up a meeting with the local parks and recreation director to share their research. Diego shared what it's like for him not to have a pool in our neighborhood. Christian talked about Kansas City's unique chapter in the desegregation of public swimming pools across our nation. Javi explained San Diego's portable pool program, demonstrating that this isn't as risky or untried as it might first appear. "I've got goose bumps," the parks and recreation director replied. They continued, "I've been in this industry for more than twenty years, and this is the single best idea that anyone has ever brought to me before. Can you please come and present at our January board meeting? We need to get these portable pools before any other department in the metro area gets them." They had done it. They had brought fresh energy and innovation to ideas that city leaders had thought were so intractable they'd thrown up their arms in despair.

The youth gave another compelling presentation to the parks and recreation board that January. It was, however, January 2020, just a few months before the world shut down and shrunk into scarcity mindsets. Now that the smoke has cleared and there's more appetite for thinking outside of mere survival, the kids are at it again, pushing their dreams forward and finding new traction.

This is why I love dead ends. When it feels like there is no way out, God makes a way out of no way. There are tools and methodologies that can be useful guides to point us in the right direction. But like every good fairy tale, if there is an honest confrontation with the forces of evil, there is no map. There is no guide to defeating them. Victory comes to those humble enough to realize that it is possible only because of unearned, hidden gifts given freely from outside of themselves. It's in those dark corners, with our backs against the wall, that God gives us light.

Eight

Some (Im)practical Advice

Jason Lief

I hear it all the time: young people don't want abstract ideas; they need something practical. We live in an age of "doing something." No one wants to read books or talk about ideas; we need to get out there and get something done. What if this is bad advice? What if the obsession to "do something" misses the mark because we don't have the slightest clue what needs to be done? Or what if we lack the imagination to try something no one has ever tried before? The problem with the current understanding of and obsession with "the practical" is it remains caught in the parameters of the way things are, leaving little possibility for something totally new—something surprising. Author Nassim Taleb refers to unpredictable events that bring change as "Black Swans."[1] These are events that could not be predicted; they lie outside the conventional wisdom and perceived knowledge of the way the world is. These events are both positive and negative, but they are understood only in hindsight. The rise of Hitler, the 9/11 attacks, the success of Google, the development of the iPhone—these are all unpredictable events that radically changed the world. A characteristic of a Black Swan is the way experts read necessity and inevitability back into their development, as if they should have been predicted. This is merely an attempt to bring the chaotic rupture of the event into the sphere of objective knowledge. But this is the wrong approach. What brings change and transformation is not what we know but what we don't know—what's yet to be discovered.

Youth ministry should focus less on order, certainty, and young people fitting into the way the world is and focus more on the beautiful chaos that is the source of life. So much time is spent on programs, curriculum, and faith formation that there's very little attention given to the conditions that bring forth change and transformation—chaos, uncertainty, and healthy bouts of stress. The current epidemic of anxiety and depression (which is very real and painful) could, in part, be the consequence of an overmanicured life. Maybe the well-intentioned attempts by adults to prevent young people from having to struggle or suffer have contributed to their fragility. At the same time, the version of faith youth leaders have been handing out isn't a biblical faith but a twenty-first-century North American faith that fits nicely within the social world as it already exists. Even the ideas of transformation and mission get co-opted to provide a sense of meaning and purpose, while very little transformation takes place.

In the Beginning . . .

The biblical story begins not with order but with chaos. When Genesis 1:1 is preached or taught, the focus tends to be on what happens next—the ordering of creation by God's word. Sure, the text begins with chaos, but we're more comfortable with the idea that God brings order. I wonder, however, if we miss something by moving too quickly to the end. Creation begins with chaos, which means life is born from the unexpected. Again and again in the biblical story, it is from a place or space where life doesn't exist that life explodes in all of its strange complexity, forged from chaotic darkness and difficult circumstances.

Abraham and Sarah are called to a place they don't know and told they're going to have descendants only to discover they can't have kids, and when they finally have a son, God tells Abraham to sacrifice him! Israel is born in suffering, brought to life through darkness, death, and a time of wandering in a barren wasteland. At the very center of Christian faith is the crucifixion of Jesus Christ, the culmination of darkness, chaos, and death found throughout the biblical story. Even baptism, the rite of initiation into the Christian community, is grounded in the symbols of chaos that connect back to Genesis 1 and the exodus, as humans are symbolically transformed as we are brought through the chaotic water. In contrast, there's a tendency in the Christian community to make sure young people have the right beliefs. This contributes to a religious perspective that focuses on young people achieving what the dominant culture holds to be the good life, one that is undergirded and guaranteed by the sprinkling on of faith.

The biblical story is consistent—true life is found by making our way through the chaos. Through the wilderness, Israel finds the promised land. Through crucifixion, the life of resurrection is possible. Only by taking up our cross do we discover eternal life. This means a life of faith is about embracing uncertainty and being willing to risk the security of the way things are for the hope of transformation.

Antifragility: Strength from Weakness

According to Nassim Taleb, to be a successful entrepreneur is to "be at some distance from expectations. The more unexpected the success of such a venture, the smaller the number of competitors, and the more successful the entrepreneur who implements the idea. . . . The payoff of a human venture is, in general, inversely proportional to what it is expected to be."[2] In his book *Antifragile: Things That Gain from Disorder*, Taleb makes the case for a national entrepreneur day to honor those who tried and failed to create something new. He suggests entrepreneurs be given the same respect and honor as soldiers who risk their lives on the battlefield. He suggests this message for the national entrepreneur day: "Most of you will fail, disrespected, impoverished, but we are grateful for the risks you are taking, and the sacrifices you are making for the sake of the economic growth of the planet and pulling others out of poverty. You are at the source of our antifragility. Our nation thanks you."[3] For Taleb, antifragility is that which embraces volatility and uncertainty while living into the stressors that come with it. Just as our bones need resistance to stay strong, our human identity needs to face trials and failure and be open to new possibilities to develop strength. Youth ministry can help young people grow resilient by inviting them into a way of discipleship that enters the difficulties and hardships of this world. It can do this not by giving them the right answers or over-spiritualizing faith but by walking with them through the hard parts of life so they might learn to embrace their humanity in Jesus Christ.

In 2 Corinthians, Paul speaks of his own hardships and suffering. He writes, "So I will boast all the more gladly of my weaknesses, so that the power of Christ may dwell in me. Therefore, I am content with weaknesses, insults, hardships, persecutions, and calamities for the sake of Christ, for whenever I am weak, then I am strong" (2 Cor 12:9–10 NRSVUE). Too often, this verse and the idea of weakness are interpreted as being about persecution for theological or moral beliefs. Christians assume this verse has nothing to do with the other aspects of our lives, just our spiritual beliefs. Yet Paul's letters to the Corinthians demonstrate how the gospel goes much deeper and penetrates our human identity in this world. When failure is no longer synonymous with shame and status is no longer determinative of worth, it frees us to imaginatively engage with the world. We are free to move through death to new forms of life, recognizing that weakness becomes the foundation for strength and courage to live as the new humanity of Jesus Christ.

Too often, youth ministry doesn't recognize the true focus of the gospel. It's not just about some world to come (although that certainly is part of it); it is about what it means to live in this world as the new humanity of Jesus Christ, loving God and loving our neighbor. The point isn't to help young people be more spiritual or moral in this world; it's to help them transform this world. Youth ministry is not about helping young people add spirituality and morality to all the other stuff they're doing; it's to help them realize how the gospel changes the way we see and interact with all the other stuff, transforming our identities so we might become signs of God's transformation.

This is where social entrepreneurship can help youth ministry regain a proper biblical focus. The point isn't to find economic security, get rich, or become famous; the point is to cultivate change and, in doing so, discover our humanity. Bringing youth ministry into conversation with social entrepreneurship provides an opportunity to help young people embrace the chaos and let go of the unhealthy obsession with "God's plan for our lives." It's an invitation for young people to exchange a domesticated religion for a life open to the possibility of what God is creating and transforming this world to be. Through this discussion, the Christian community can reframe failure as part of the human condition, inviting young people to embrace weakness and cultivate antifragility. This is the point, really: equipping young people to become human beings with the courage to live into the beautiful diversity and insecurity of life.

So what does this mean for your ministry? I wish I knew. But that's the point—the gospel calls us into the unknown of our lives with nothing but faith, hope, and love. Hopefully, these insights and stories can spark creativity as you bring the gospel into conversation with the lived experiences of young people and the needs of the world.

Acknowledgments

Writing a book is the culmination of many conversations with people who are both dead and alive. To begin I must say that I'm grateful Kurt agreed to write this book with me. Over the past ten years, we've had many conversations about immigration and community development, usually on the front porch of his parent's house in Argentine. He's quick to tell people to be careful when they talk to me—I might ask them to cowrite a book. I'm thankful for my work with the National Immigration Forum, which has provided me with new insights into the needs of my community and led to a wonderful partnership with Martha Draayer and the people at Maria Magdalena Church. When I started this book, the church didn't exist; now, the ideas from this book are coming to life as we imagine what flourishing looks like in Northwest Iowa. I'm grateful to students and colleagues at Northwestern College for the opportunity to teach and discuss ideas. Our conversations functioned as incubators in which I was able to try out and revise ideas through a wonderful back-and-forth. Regarding the publishing of this book, I want to say thank you to Beth Gaede, who said "yes" to our project, and to Bethany Dickerson, who brought it to life.

In many ways, this book—my part of it, anyway—comes from an engagement with a supportive community. The beautiful people of "Old Town" Sioux Center offer both critiques and encouragement. Laremy and Rebecca De Vries, the philosopher-entrepreneurs, have created an unrivaled communal space in the Fruited Plain Café. Luke and Sara Hawley are positive examples of ingenuity and reclamation. Dave and Emily Kramer provide a both historical and scientific mode of being that reminds us of where we've been and the new possibilities that await us. The Old Town wild horde of children, with their spunk and imagination, give me hope for the future of humanity. Where would I be without Mark Tazelaar and Paul Fessler? Mark is a philosopher, financial adviser, and friend. He is a gracious Nietzschean, enthusiastically supporting my endeavors while honestly letting me know when the title we've chosen is terrible. Paul reminds me to listen to the other side of an argument, to be gracious and hospitable, and to fight against the monopoly of MLB.tv. (Iowa is the black hole of MLB.tv, as six teams are blacked out.)

As a kid, I remember hearing my grandpa Lief and my dad tell stories about the crazy businesses they wanted to start but never did. They possessed an entrepreneurial spirit that never came to fruition. I've inherited this spirit, and this book is hopefully a reflection of this Liefish trait—for good and for bad. So, I'm grateful to my parents, Dave and Sandy, and my extended family for teaching me it's OK to color outside the lines. Finally, I would like to thank my beautiful wife, Tamara, and my loving children—Naomi, Christian, and Savannah—for letting me disappear to the cabin to get some writing done. And for Lady and Meow Meow, valiant guardians of the Lief homestead from the mailman's diabolical plan to conquer the tristate area—I am forever grateful.

Jason Lief

I would not be the person that I am today without my friends and neighbors first in Pesqueria, Nuevo Leon, and now in the Argentine neighborhood of Kansas City, Kansas. While almost always short on cash and low in status, they are rich in culture and vibrant in character. I've learned so much standing in solidarity with you. Together, we've lifted up valleys and made mountains low. I wouldn't want to be anywhere else.

I want to thank all of the ImagineX crews who dared to turn their faces toward the pain in our neighborhood and imagine what it looks like when heaven comes to earth. I especially want to thank Elizabeth, Nancy, Rhiannon, and Zaira, who started it all when neither you nor I had any idea what we were doing—until Esteban Garcia, fresh off a flight from Spain, stepped in to save the day. Special thanks to Kenny Clewett for scheming with me from the beginning and—as all good teachers do—leaving me flailing in the deep end to figure out how to relax and tread water on my own. Kenny kept the Madrid-to-KC pipeline going strong with support from Simon Menendez and Cristina Garcia, who taught us that we could not only tread water; we could fly. Thanks to Kelli Schutte for start-up funding and strategic conversations and to Kevin for nearly two decades of friendship and shared imagination for God's kingdom.

I'm so grateful to Youthfront for giving me a long leash, for trusting in me. Innovation requires the fortitude to weather strikeouts on the path to increased slugging percentages. Mike King still puts me out on the plate, and I'm grateful. Amber Booth has been a great friend and an amazing collaborator and organizer in all of our dreams for a better world. Erik Leafblad—in addition to being one of my dearest friends—has lent me one of the sharpest theological minds I've encountered and has made sure God's good news spills out onto the streets around us. I can't leave out Alain Olivo and Rodolfo Armendariz, who have journeyed with me outside the camp and have been important conversation partners in imagining God's kingdom in spite of the brokenness we see before us. Thanks to Jason for believing this worthy of being turned into a book and for his friendship and conspiratorial partnership in seeking goodness for those on the margins of our communities.

Finally, I want to thank my family. There are many parents who would do everything in their power to dissuade their children from leaving a charmed, rural life in Northwest Iowa for one on the poor outskirts of a Mexican metropolis or a working-class immigrant neighborhood with criminal reputations. Neither my parents nor my in-laws are those kinds of parents. They have been the best supporters, cheerleaders, and collaborators in mending God's world that we could have asked for. Emily, you're the one for me. We had no idea where this road would take us. When we happened upon those bread-crumb trails in the forest leading to what was next, I was the one who naively and eagerly followed, typically getting us both into trouble. But it's you who pushes the witch into the oven, turning nightmares into fairy tales that bless everyone around us. And finally, thank you to our sons—Luke, Perkins, and Leo—who have been the very best collaborators, wishing to live nowhere else, innovating a very good life in one of the unlikeliest of places.

Kurt Rietema

Notes

Chapter One: Youth Ministry Must Die

1 Kenda Creasy Dean et al., *Delighted: What Teenagers Are Teaching the Church about Joy* (Grand Rapids, MI: Wm. B. Eerdmans, 2020); David Kinnaman, Mark Matlock, and Aly Hawkins, *Faith for Exiles: 5 Ways for a New Generation to Follow Jesus in Digital Babylon* (Grand Rapids, MI: Baker Books, 2019); Kara Powell, Jake Mulder, and Brad Griffin, *Growing Young: Six Essential Strategies to Help Young People Discover and Love Your Church* (Grand Rapids, MI: Baker Books, 2016).

2 Charles Taylor, *A Secular Age* (Cambridge, MA: Belknap Press of Harvard University Press, 2007).

3 Pete Davis, *Dedicated: The Case for Commitment in an Age of Infinite Browsing* (New York: Avid Reader, 2021), 10.

4 "BBC Two—Extreme Pilgrim, Egypt: The Desert," BBC, accessed March 11, 2022, https://www.bbc.co.uk/programmes/b008pxlz.

5 "Social Entrepreneurship: The Case for Definition," SSIR, accessed August 27, 2020, https://ssir.org/articles/entry/social_entrepreneurship _the_case_for_definition.

6 "Social Entrepreneurship."

7 Mark Sampson, "The Promise (and Peril) of Missional Entrepreneurship," *ANVIL* 33, no. 1 (April 2017): 3.

8 Sampson.

9 Sampson. See also Pope Benedict XVI, *Charity in Truth* (San Francisco: Ignatius, 2009).

10 Sampson, "Promise," 7.

Chapter Two: Disconnection

1 "Joker (2019)," IMDb, accessed March 11, 2022, https://www.imdb .com/title/tt7286456/.

2 Melinda Lundquist Denton, Richard Flory, and Christian Smith, *Back-Pocket God: Religion and Spirituality in the Lives of Emerging Adults* (New York: Oxford University Press, 2020), 16.

3 Denton, Flory, and Smith, 41–42.

4 Denton, Flory, and Smith, 42.

5 Denton, Flory, and Smith, 150.

6 Denton, Flory, and Smith, 232–33.

7 Kathryn Tanner, *Economy of Grace* (Minneapolis: Fortress, 2005), 84.

8 Zygmunt Bauman, *Consuming Life* (Hoboken, NJ: John Wiley & Sons, 2013), 57.

9 Malcolm Harris, *Kids These Days: Human Capital and the Making of Millennials* (Boston: Little, Brown, 2017), 5.

10 Harris, 6.

11 Harris, 7.

12 Harris, 14.

13 Harris, 39.

14 "Hunt for the Wilderpeople (2016)," IMDb, accessed April 9, 2022, https://www.imdb.com/title/tt4698684/.

15 Wendy Wood, *Good Habits, Bad Habits: The Science of Making Positive Changes That Stick* (New York: Farrar, Straus and Giroux, 2019), 9.

16 Wood, 10.

17 For a more in-depth discussion of this passage, see Jean-Luc Marion, "They Recognized Him; and He Became Invisible to Them," *Modern Theology* 18, no. 2 (December 17, 2002): 145–52.

18 Jürgen Moltmann, *The Way of Jesus Christ: Christology in Messianic Dimensions* (Minneapolis: Fortress, 1995).

Chapter Three: Reconnection

1 John Chryssavgis, *In the Heart of the Desert: The Spirituality of the Desert Fathers and Mothers* (Bloomington, IN: World Wisdom, 2008), 2.
2 Chryssavgis, 17.
3 Chryssavgis, 33–34.
4 Chryssavgis, 38.
5 Joan Chittister, *In God's Holy Light: Wisdom from the Desert Monastics* (Cincinnati: Franciscan Media, 2015), 37.
6 Chittister, 38.
7 Chittister, 39.
8 Chittister, 39.
9 Chittister, 12.
10 Chittister, 12.
11 Chittister, 108.
12 Chittister, 109.
13 See Daniel C. Dennett, *Consciousness Explained*, 1st ed. (Boston: Back Bay Books, 1992).
14 Rowan Williams, *Being Human: Bodies, Minds, Persons* (Grand Rapids, MI: Wm. B. Eerdmans, 2018), 8.
15 Williams, 9.
16 Williams, 11.
17 Williams, 31.

Chapter Four: Seeking the Welfare of the City

1 Mary Schmich, "'Vulnerable' Cafe Makes a Stand in a Tough Part of Town," *Chicago Tribune*, November 20, 2014, https://www.chicagotribune.com/columns/mary-schmich/ct-kusanya-cafe-englewood-schmich-met-1121-20141120-column.html.
2 Elaine Graham, *Transforming Practice: Pastoral Theology in an Age of Uncertainty* (Eugene, OR: Wipf & Stock, 2002), 7.
3 Graham, 7.

4 Richard R. Osmer, *Practical Theology: An Introduction* (Grand Rapids, MI: Wm. B. Eerdmans, 2008), 4.

5 Osmer, 4.

6 Osmer, 4.

7 Osmer, 4.

8 Roger L. Martin and Sally Osberg, *Getting beyond Better: How Social Entrepreneurship Works* (Boston: Harvard Business Review Press, 2015), 18–19.

9 Jacques Ellul, *The Meaning of the City* (Eugene, OR: Wipf & Stock, 2011).

Chapter Five: Going Off Script with God's Mission

1 Peter Block, *Community: The Structure of Belonging* (Oakland: Berrett-Koehler, 2009).

2 Gilbert Rosenthal, "Tikkun ha-Olam: The Metamorphosis of a Concept," *Journal of Religion* 85, no. 2 (April 2005): 219.

Chapter Six: Confronting Adult-Sized Problems

1 Robert D. Putnam, *Our Kids: The American Dream in Crisis* (New York: Simon & Schuster, 2016).

2 Ashley Z. Hand and Michael Peterson, *Report on 2023 Community Input* (Kansas City: Unified Government of Wyandotte County, 2022), 19, https://www.wycokck.org/files/assets/public/finance/documents/budget/dotte-talk-2023_community-budget-input_2022.06.16.pdf?fbclid=IwAR0b82G_jW4o3NsFNA9PBe_gRmV5zsaNKrljbDUu7Q-9TOOcw9t34ogMpp0.

3 Gordon Cosby, "The Radical Vision of the Church of the Savior," in *Tell the Word* (Washington, DC: Church of the Savior), 4, https://s3.amazonaws.com/dfc_attachments/public/documents/3215434/Journey_Inward__Outward_and_Forward_The_Radical_Vision_of_the_Church_of_the_Saviour.pdf.

4 Tina Fey, *Bossypants* (Boston: Little, Brown, 2013), 85.

5 *Dead Poets Society*, directed by Peter Weir, produced by Steven Haft (United States: Touchstone Pictures, 1989).

Chapter Seven: Creating toward God's Future

1 *Back to the Future II*, directed by Robert Zemeckis (United States: Universal Pictures, 1989).

2 Mike Sherry, "Figures Reveal Racial Divide in Swimming Pool Deaths," KCUR, August 7, 2014, https://www.kcur.org/health/2014-08-07/figures-reveal-racial-divide-in-swimming-pool-deaths#stream/0.

3 Jeff Wiltse, *Contested Waters: A Social History of Swimming Pools in America* (Chapel Hill: University of North Carolina Press, 2007).

4 James K. A. Smith, *You Are What You Love: The Spiritual Power of Habit* (Grand Rapids, MI: Brazos, 2016); James K. A. Smith, *Desiring the Kingdom (Cultural Liturgies): Worship, Worldview, and Cultural Formation* (Grand Rapids, MI: Baker Academic, 2009).

5 Smith, *You Are What You Love*, 9.

6 Smith, 16.

7 Smith, 9.

8 Stanley Hauerwas and William H. Willimon, *Resident Aliens: Life in the Christian Colony* (Nashville: Abingdon, 2004).

9 Smith, *Desiring the Kingdom*, 42.

10 National Civil Rights Meeting, "Proceedings of the Civil Rights Mass-Meeting Held at Lincoln Hall, October 22, 1883. Speeches of Hon. Frederick Douglass and Robert G. Ingersoll," Frederick Douglass Papers at the Library of Congress, Washington, DC, October 22, 1883, https://udspace.udel.edu/handle/19716/21266.

11 Mark Vonnegut, *The Eden Express: A Memoir of Insanity* (New York: Seven Stories, 1975).

12 Saint Irenaeus, Bishop of Lyon, *Libros quinque adversus haereses*, Greek and Latin ed. (Cambridge: Typis academicis, 1857).

13 Smith, *You Are What You Love*, 56.

14 Andrew Root, *Churches and the Crisis of Decline: A Hopeful, Practical Ecclesiology for a Secular Age*, Ministry in a Secular Age 4 (Grand Rapids, MI: Baker Academic, 2022), 143.

15 Root, 143, 147.

16 "History of Parks' Swimming Pools," New York City Department of Parks & Recreation, accessed November 1, 2022, https://www .nycgovparks.org/about/history/pools.

Chapter Eight: Some (Im)practical Advice

1 Nassim Nicholas Taleb, *The Black Swan: The Impact of the Highly Improbable*, 2nd ed., with a new section, "On Robustness and Fragility" (New York: Random House, 2010).

2 Taleb, xxiv.

3 Nassim Nicholas Taleb, *Antifragile: Things That Gain from Disorder* (New York: Random House, 2012), 80.

Selected Bibliography

Bauman, Zygmunt. *Consuming Life*. Hoboken, NJ: John Wiley & Sons, 2013.

BBC. "BBC Two—Extreme Pilgrim, Egypt: The Desert." Accessed March 11, 2022. https://www.bbc.co.uk/programmes/b008pxlz.

Chittister, Joan. *In God's Holy Light: Wisdom from the Desert Monastics*. Cincinnati: Franciscan Media, 2015.

Chryssavgis, John. *In the Heart of the Desert: The Spirituality of the Desert Fathers and Mothers*. Bloomington, IN: World Wisdom, 2008.

Cosby, Gordon. "The Radical Vision of the Church of the Savior." In *Tell the Word*, 4. Washington, DC: Church of the Savior. https://s3 .amazonaws.com/dfc_attachments/public/documents/3215434/ Journey_Inward__Outward_and_Forward_The_Radical_Vision_of _the_Church_of_the_Saviour.pdf.

Davis, Pete. *Dedicated: The Case for Commitment in an Age of Infinite Browsing*. New York: Avid Reader, 2021.

Dean, Kenda Creasy, Wesley W. Ellis, Justin Forbes, and Abigail Visco Rusert. *Delighted: What Teenagers Are Teaching the Church about Joy*. Grand Rapids, MI: Wm. B. Eerdmans, 2020.

Dennett, Daniel C. *Consciousness Explained*. 1st ed. Boston: Back Bay Books, 1992.

Denton, Melinda Lundquist, Richard Flory, and Christian Smith. *Back-Pocket God: Religion and Spirituality in the Lives of Emerging Adults*. New York: Oxford University Press, 2020.

Ellul, Jacques. *The Meaning of the City*. Eugene, OR: Wipf & Stock, 2011.

Fey, Tina. *Bossypants*. Boston: Little, Brown, 2013.

Graham, Elaine. *Transforming Practice: Pastoral Theology in an Age of Uncertainty*. Eugene, OR: Wipf & Stock, 2002.

Hand, Ashley Z., and Michael Peterson. *Report on 2023 Community Input*. Kansas City: Unified Government of Wyandotte County, 2022. https://www.wycokck.org/files/assets/public/finance/documents/budget/dotte-talk-2023_community-budget-input_2022.06.16.pdf?fbclid=IwAR0b82G_jW4o3NsFNA9PBe_gRmV5zsaNKrljbDUu7Q-9T00cw9t34ogMpp0.

Harris, Malcolm. *Kids These Days: Human Capital and the Making of Millennials*. Boston: Little, Brown, 2017.

Hauerwas, Stanley, and Bishop William H. Willimon. *Resident Aliens: Life in the Christian Colony*. Nashville: Abingdon, 2004.

IMDb. "Back to the Future Part II (1989)." Accessed November 1, 2022. https://www.imdb.com/title/tt0096874/?ref_=fn_al_tt_4.

———. "Hunt for the Wilderpeople (2016)." Accessed April 9, 2022. https://www.imdb.com/title/tt4698684/.

———. "Joker (2019)." Accessed March 11, 2022. https://www.imdb.com/title/tt7286456/.

KCUR 89.3—NPR in Kansas City. "Figures Reveal Racial Divide in Swimming Pool Deaths." August 7, 2014. https://www.kcur.org/health/2014-08-07/figures-reveal-racial-divide-in-swimming-pool-deaths.

Kinnaman, David, Mark Matlock, and Aly Hawkins. *Faith for Exiles: 5 Ways for a New Generation to Follow Jesus in Digital Babylon*. Grand Rapids, MI: Baker Books, 2019.

Marion, Jean-Luc. "They Recognized Him; and He Became Invisible to Them." *Modern Theology* 18, no. 2 (December 17, 2002): 145–152.

Martin, Roger L., and Sally Osberg. *Getting beyond Better: How Social Entrepreneurship Works.* Boston: Harvard Business Review Press, 2015.

National Civil Rights Meeting. "Proceedings of the Civil Rights Mass-Meeting Held at Lincoln Hall, October 22, 1883. Speeches of Hon. Frederick Douglass and Robert G. Ingersoll." Frederick Douglass Papers at the Library of Congress, Washington, DC, October 22, 1883. https://udspace.udel.edu/handle/19716/21266.

New York City Department of Parks & Recreation. "History of Parks' Swimming Pools." Accessed November 1, 2022. https://www.nycgovparks.org/about/history/pools.

Osmer, Richard R. *Practical Theology: An Introduction.* Grand Rapids, MI: Wm. B. Eerdmans, 2008.

Pope Benedict XVI. *Charity in Truth.* San Francisco: Ignatius, 2009.

Powell, Kara, Jake Mulder, and Brad Griffin. *Growing Young: Six Essential Strategies to Help Young People Discover and Love Your Church.* Grand Rapids, MI: Baker Books, 2016.

Putnam, Robert D. *Our Kids: The American Dream in Crisis.* New York: Simon & Schuster, 2016.

Root, Andrew. *Churches and the Crisis of Decline: A Hopeful, Practical Ecclesiology for a Secular Age.* Ministry in a Secular Age 4. Grand Rapids, MI: Baker Academic, 2022.

Saint Irenaeus, Bishop of Lyon. *Libros quinque adversus haereses.* Greek and Latin ed. Cambridge: Typis academicis, 1857.

Sampson, Mark. "The Promise (and Peril) of Missional Entrepreneurship." *ANVIL* 33, no. 1: 4–11.

Schmich, Mary. "'Vulnerable' Cafe Makes a Stand in a Tough Part of Town." *Chicago Tribune*, November 20, 2014. https://www.chicagotribune.com/columns/mary-schmich/ct-kusanya-cafe-englewood-schmich-met-1121-20141120-column.html.

Smith, James K. A. *You Are What You Love: The Spiritual Power of Habit*. Grand Rapids, MI: Brazos, 2016.

SSIR. "Social Entrepreneurship: The Case for Definition." Accessed August 27, 2020. https://ssir.org/articles/entry/social_entrepreneurship_the_case_for_definition.

Taleb, Nassim Nicholas. *Antifragile: Things That Gain from Disorder*. New York: Random House, 2012.

———. *The Black Swan: The Impact of the Highly Improbable*. 2nd ed., with a new section, "On Robustness and Fragility." New York: Random House, 2010.

Tanner, Kathryn. *Economy of Grace*. Minneapolis: Fortress, 2005.

Taylor, Charles. *A Secular Age*. Cambridge, MA: Belknap Press of Harvard University Press, 2007.

Vonnegut, Mark. *The Eden Express: A Memoir of Insanity*. New York: Seven Stories, 1975.

Weir, Peter, dir. *Dead Poets Society*. Produced by Steven Haft. United States: Touchstone Pictures, 1989.

Williams, Rowan. *Being Human: Bodies, Minds, Persons*. Grand Rapids, MI: Wm. B. Eerdmans, 2018.

Wiltse, Jeff. *Contested Waters: A Social History of Swimming Pools in America*. Chapel Hill: University of North Carolina Press, 2007.

Wood, Wendy. *Good Habits, Bad Habits: The Science of Making Positive Changes That Stick*. New York: Farrar, Straus and Giroux, 2019.